Global Mineral Resource Assessment

Porphyry Copper Assessment of the Tibetan Plateau, China

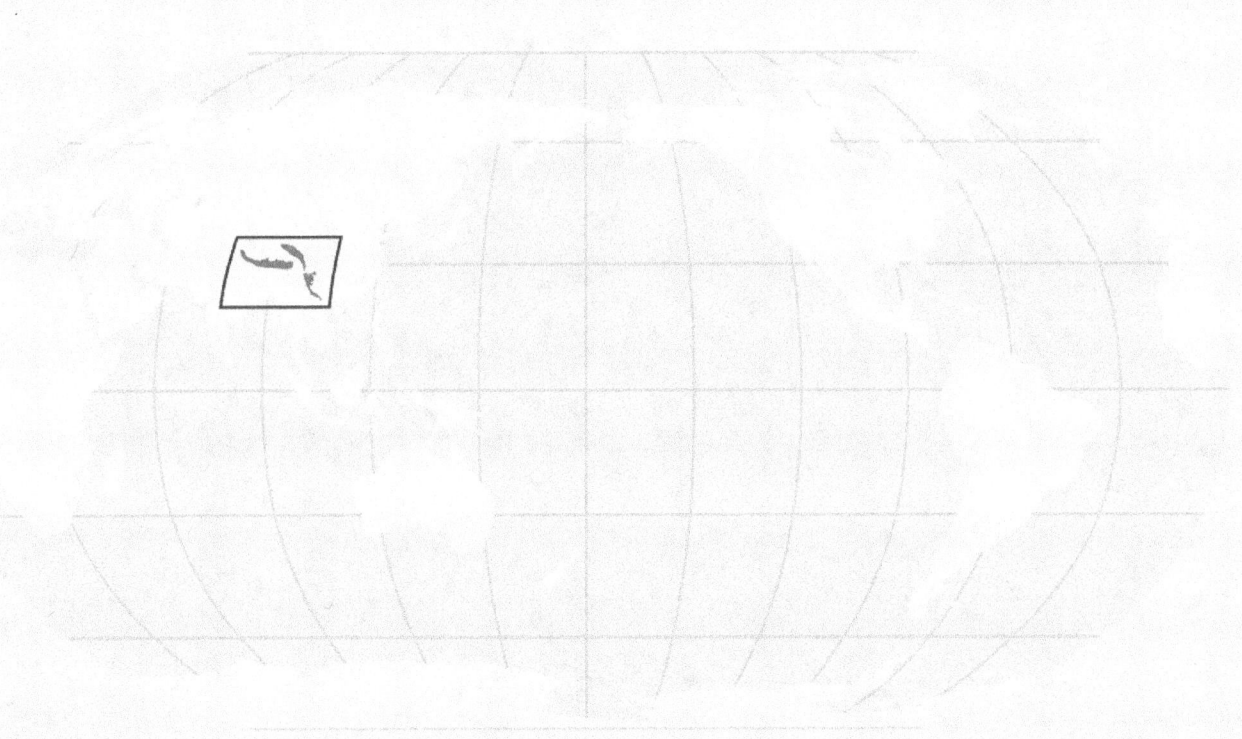

Prepared in cooperation with the China Geological Survey and the Chinese Academy of Geological Sciences

Scientific Investigations Report 2010–5090–F

U.S. Department of the Interior
U.S. Geological Survey

This page left intentionally blank.

Global Mineral Resource Assessment

Michael L. Zientek, Jane M. Hammarstrom, Kathleen M. Johnson, and Frances W. Pierce, editors

Porphyry Copper Assessment of the Tibetan Plateau, China

By Steve Ludington, Jane M. Hammarstrom, Gilpin R. Robinson, Jr., John C. Mars, and Robert J. Miller, based on contributions of Yan Guangsheng, Peng Qiuming, Lian Changyun, Mao Jingwen, Li Jinyi, Xiao Keyan, Qiu Ruizhao, Shao Jianbao, Shai Gangyi, Du Yuliang, and Dennis Cox

Prepared in cooperation with the China Geological Survey and the Chinese Academy of Geological Sciences

Scientific Investigations Report 2010–5090–F

U.S. Department of the Interior
U.S. Geological Survey

U.S. Department of the Interior
KEN SALAZAR, Secretary

U.S. Geological Survey
Marcia K. McNutt, Director

U.S. Geological Survey, Reston, Virginia: 2012

This report and any updates to it are available online at:
http://pubs.usgs.gov/sir/2010/5090/f/

For more information on the USGS—the Federal source for science about the Earth,
its natural and living resources, natural hazards, and the environment—
visit http://www.usgs.gov or call 1–888–ASK–USGS

For an overview of USGS information products, including maps, imagery, and publications,
visit http://www.usgs.gov/pubprod

Suggested citation:
Ludington, Steve, Hammarstrom, J.M., Robinson, G.R., Jr., Mars, J.C., and Miller, R.J., 2012,
Porphyry copper assessment of the Tibetan Plateau, China: U.S. Geological Survey Scientific
Investigations Report 2010–5090–F, 63 p. and GIS data.

Acknowledgments

The assessment of porphyry copper deposits on the Tibetan Plateau has a long history, and many different people have been involved. Klaus J. Schulz and Joseph A. Briskey initiated the project and participated in the first workshop, in Kunming, Yunnan, in 2002. Drs. Stephen G. Peters and Warren Nokleberg coordinated and led the initial assessment activities, prepared preliminary reports, and represented the USGS to our Chinese counterparts at several meetings. Jack H. Medlin, as USGS international specialist for Asia and the Pacific, facilitated joint project activities. Kathleen M. Johnson, USGS Mineral Resources Program Coordinator provided spirited and constant support over the life of the project. Niki E. Wintzer, Heather L. Parks, Deborah A. Briggs, and Kathleen D. Gans provided technical support.

USGS colleagues Peter Vikre, David M. Sutphin, Michael L. Zientek, and Mark J. Mihalasky served on an assessment oversight committee to evaluate the assessment results prior to publication. Stephen G. Peters provided data, expertise, and reviews of preliminary drafts of some assessment tracts.

Technical reviews of the manuscript and GIS were provided by Edward A. du Bray, Robert A. Ayuso, and Connie Dicken.

Scientists from the China Geological Survey and the Chinese Academy of Geological Sciences generously participated in assessment meetings and provided data that would not have otherwise been available. We would especially like to thank Drs. Qiu Ruizhao, Tan Yonglie, and Chen Xiufa, who accompanied the senior author on a field trip in western North America and hosted him for visits to copper deposits in China.

Contents

Figures

Tables

Acronyms and Abbreviations Used in this report

ANOVA	analysis of variance
CCOP	Coordinating Committee for Geoscience Programmes in East and Southeast Asia
CGS	China Geological Survey
GIS	Geographic Information System
GMRAP	Global Mineral Resource Assessment Project
HREE	heavy rare-earth elements
kt	thousand metric tons
LREE	light rare-earth elements
MASH	melt, assimilation, storage, and homogenization
Ma	million of years before the present
Mt	million metric tons
REE	rare-earth elements
SCLM	subcontinental lithospheric mantle
SHRIMP	sensitive high resolution ion microprobe
SSIB	small-scale digital internal boundaries
USGS	United States Geological Survey

Conversion Factors

Inch/Pound to SI	Multiply by	To obtain
	Length	
foot (ft)	0.3048	meter (m)
mile (mi)	1.609	kilometer (km)
yard (yd)	0.9144	meter (m)
	Area	
acre	4,047	square meter (m2)
acre	0.4047	hectare (ha)
acre	0.4047	square hectometer (hm2)
acre	0.004047	square kilometer (km2)
square mile (mi2)	259.0	hectare (ha)
square mile (mi2)	2.590	square kilometer (km2)
	Mass	
ounce, avoirdupois (oz)	28.35	gram (g)
pound, avoirdupois (lb)	0.4536	kilogram (kg)
ton, short (T) (2,000 lb)	0.9072	megagram (Mg)
ton, short (T) (2,000 lb.)	907.18474	kilogram (kg)
ton, short (T) (2,000 lb.)	0.90718474	metric ton (t)

SI to Inch/Pound	Multiply by	To obtain
	Length	
meter (m)	3.281	foot (ft)
kilometer (km)	0.6214	mile (mi)
meter (m)	1.094	yard (yd)
	Area	
hectare (ha)	2.471	acre
square hectometer (hm^2)	2.471	acre
square kilometer (km^2)	247.1	acre
square centimeter (cm^2)	0.001076	square foot (ft^2)
square meter (m^2)	10.76	square foot (ft^2)
square centimeter (cm^2)	0.1550	square inch (ft^2)
hectare (ha)	0.003861	square mile (mi^2)
square kilometer (km^2)	0.3861	square mile (mi^2)
	Mass	
gram (g)	0.03527	ounce, avoirdupois (oz)
kilogram (kg)	2.205	pound avoirdupois (lb)
megagram (Mg)	1.102	ton, short (2,000 lb)
megagram (Mg)	0.9842	ton, long (2,240 lb)

Chemical Symbols

Element	Symbol	Element	Symbol	Element	Symbol
Actinium	Ac	Germanium	Ge	Potassium (Kalium)	K
Aluminum	Al	Gold	Au	Praseodymium	Pr
Americum	Am	Hafnium	Hf	Promethium	Pm
Antimony (Stibium)	Sb	Helium	He	Palladium	Pa
Argon	Ar	Holmium	Ho	Radium	Ra
Arsenic	As	Hydrogen	H	Radon	Rn
Astatine	At	Indium	In	Rhenium	Re
Barium	Ba	Iodine	I	Rhodium	Rh
Berkelium	Bk	Iridium	Ir	Rubidium	Rb
Beryllium	Be	Iron	Fe	Ruthenium	Ru
Bismuth	Bi	Krypton	Kr	Samarium	Sm
Boron	B	Lanthanum	La	Scandium	Sc
Bromine	Br	Lawrencium	Lr	Selenium	Se
Cadmium	Cd	Lead	Pb	Silicon	Si
Cesium	Cs	Lithium	Li	Silver	Ag
Calcium	Ca	Lutetium	Lu	Sodium (Natrium)	Na
Californium	Cf	Magnesium	Mg	Strontium	Sr
Carbon	C	Manganese	Mn	Sulfur	S
Cerium	Ce	Mendelveium	Md	Tantalum	Ta
Chlorine	Cl	Mercury	Hg	Technetium	Tc
Chromium	Cr	Molybdenum	Mo	Tellurium	Te
Cobalt	Co	Neodymium	Nd	Terbium	Tb
Copper	Cu	Neon	Ne	Thallium	Tl
Curium	Cm	Neptunium	Np	Tungsten (Wolfram)	W
Dysprosium	Dy	Nickel	Ni	(Unnihexium)	(Unh)
Eisteinium	Es	Niobium	Nb	(Unnilpentium)	(Unp)
Erbium	Er	Nitrogen	N	(Unnilquadium)	(Unq)
Europium	Eu	Nobelium	No	Uranium	U
Fermium	Fm	Osmium	Os	Vanadium	V
Fluorine	Fm	Oxygen	Os	Xenon	Xe
Francium	Fr	Palladium	Pd	Ytterbium	Yb
Gadolinium	Gd	Phosphorus	P	Yttrium	Y
Gallium	Ga	Platinum	Pt	Zinc	Zn
				Zirconium	Zr

Porphyry Copper Assessment of the Tibetan Plateau, China

By Steve Ludington[1], Jane M. Hammarstrom[2], Gilpin R. Robinson, Jr.[2], John C. Mars[2], and Robert J. Miller[1], based on contributions of Yan Guangsheng[3], Peng Qiuming[3], Lian Changyun[3], Mao Jingwen[4], Li Jinyi[3], Xiao Keyan[3], Qiu Ruizhao[3], Shao Jianbao[3], Shai Gangyi[3], Du Yuliang[3], and Dennis Cox[1]

Abstract

The U.S. Geological Survey collaborated with the China Geological Survey to conduct a mineral-resource assessment of resources in porphyry copper deposits on the Tibetan Plateau in western China. This area hosts several very large porphyry deposits, exemplified by the Yulong and Qulong deposits, each containing at least 7,000,000 metric tons (t) of copper. However, large parts of the area are underexplored and are likely to contain undiscovered porphyry copper deposits.

Three tracts were delineated as permissive for porphyry copper deposits on the Tibetan Plateau—the Yulong (Eocene and Oligocene), Dali (Eocene through Miocene), and Gangdese (Oligocene and Miocene) tracts. The tracts were defined based on mapped and inferred subsurface distributions of igneous rocks of specific age ranges in which the occurrence of porphyry copper deposits is possible. These tracts range in area from about 95,000 to about 240,000 square kilometers. Although maps of different scales were used in the assessment, the final tract boundaries are intended for use at a scale of 1:1,000,000.

The deposits on the Tibetan Plateau all formed in a post-subduction environment, one newly recognized as permissive for the occurrence of porphyry copper deposits. Based on the grade, tonnage, and geologic characteristics of the known deposits, two tracts, Yulong and Gangdese, were evaluated using the general (Cu-Mo-Au) porphyry copper grade and tonnage model. The Dali tract was evaluated using the gold-rich (Cu-Au) submodel. Assessment participants estimated numbers of undiscovered deposits at different levels of confidence for each permissive tract. These estimates were then combined with the selected grade and tonnage models using Monte Carlo simulation to generate quantitative probabilistic estimates of undiscovered resources. Additional resources in extensions of deposits with identified resources were not specifically evaluated.

Assessment results, presented in tables and graphs, show mean expected amounts of metal and rock in undiscovered deposits at different quantile levels, as well as the arithmetic mean for each tract. This assessment estimated a mean of 39 undiscovered porphyry copper deposits within the assessed permissive tracts on the Tibetan Plateau. This represents nearly four times the number of known deposits (11) already discovered. Predicted mean (arithmetic) resources that could be associated with the undiscovered deposits are about 145,000,000 t of copper and about 4,900 t of gold, as well as byproduct molybdenum and silver. Reliable reports of the identified resources in the 11 known deposits total about 27,000,000 t of copper and about 800 t of gold. Therefore, based on the assessments of undiscovered Tibetan Plateau resources in this report, about six times as much copper may occur in undiscovered porphyry copper deposits as has been identified to date.

Introduction

Cenozoic deposits on the Tibetan Plateau of western China constitute one of the world's important emerging copper provinces. This area hosts at least two world class deposits, Yulong and Qulong, at least nine other porphyry copper deposits (table 1), and numerous prospects and related deposits (fig. 1). Yulong, which contains at least 7,000,000 metric tons (t) of copper, was discovered in the late 1960s (Gu and others, 2003); soon thereafter, many additional outcropping deposits were discovered in the Yulong belt. Qulong, which also contains more than 7,000,000 t of copper, was discovered during regional stream-sediment geochemical studies in the late 1980s (Yang and others, 2009), and additional discoveries continue. Most of the deposits in this area contain important amounts of molybdenum, gold, and silver, all of which will likely be important byproducts.

Copper production commenced at Yulong in late 2008 and at Jiama in July of 2010. Other deposits are in advanced stages of development. The high altitude, remote location, and lack of infrastructure in the region pose serious challenges to mineral exploitation in the region.

The U.S. Geological Survey (USGS) conducted a probabilistic mineral resource assessment of undiscovered resources in porphyry copper deposits on the Tibetan Plateau as part of a global mineral resource assessment project (GMRAP). The purpose of the assessment was to (1) compile a database of known porphyry copper deposits and significant prospects, (2) delineate permissive areas (tracts) for undiscovered porphyry copper deposits at a scale of 1:1,000,000, (3) estimate numbers of undiscovered deposits within those permissive tracts, and (4) provide probabilistic estimates of amounts of copper (Cu), molybdenum (Mo), gold (Au), and silver (Ag) that could be contained in those undiscovered deposits. The study was conducted in cooperation with the China Geological Survey (CGS) between 2002 and 2010. The part of the

---

[1]U.S. Geological Survey, Menlo Park, California, United States.

[2]U.S. Geological Survey, Reston, Virginia, United States.

[3]China Geological Survey, Beijing, China.

[4]Chinese Academy of Geological Sciences, Beijing, China.

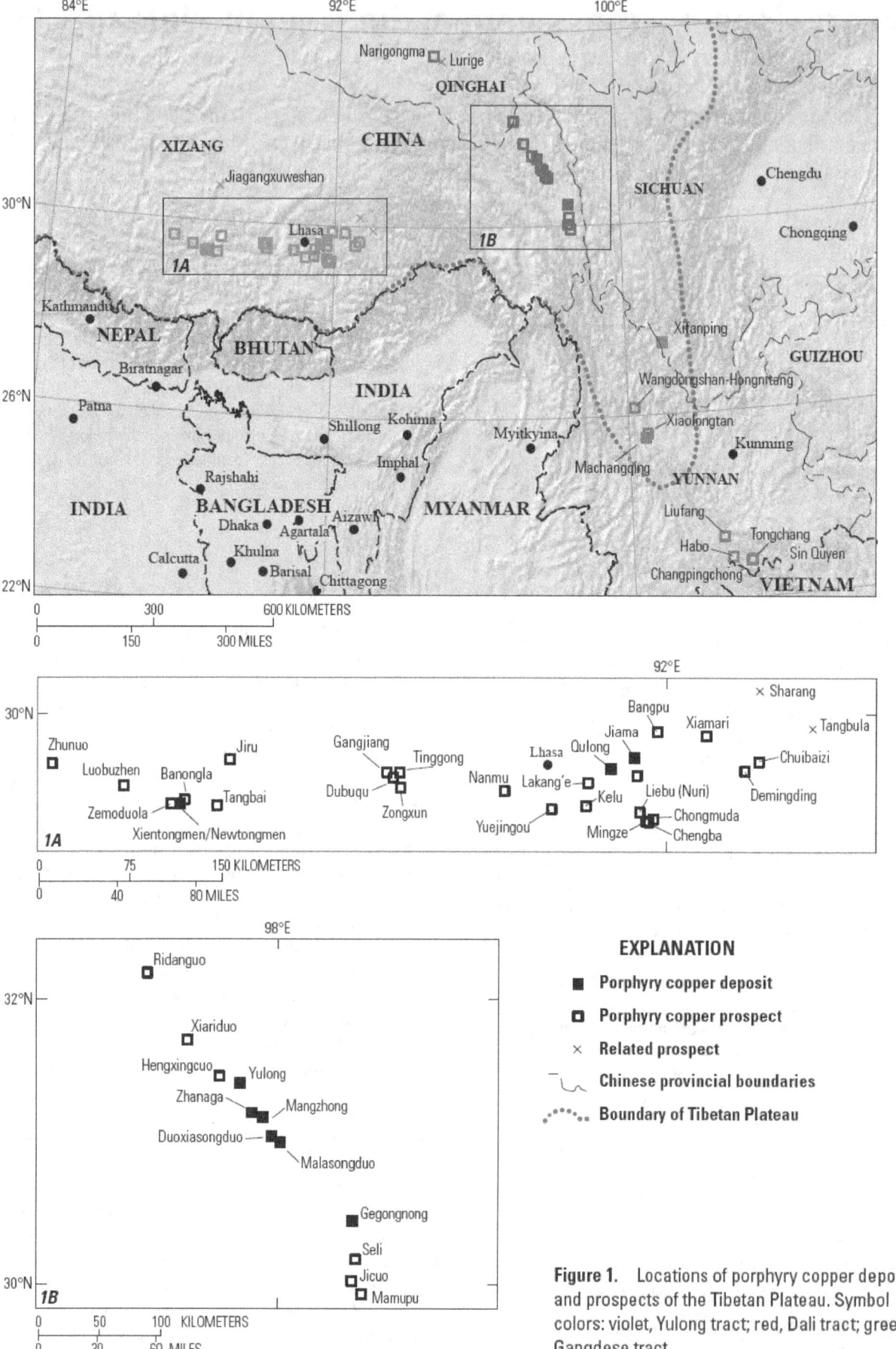

Figure 1. Locations of porphyry copper deposits and prospects of the Tibetan Plateau. Symbol colors: violet, Yulong tract; red, Dali tract; green, Gangdese tract.

Table 1. Summary of identified resources in porphyry copper deposits of the Tibetan Plateau

[Ma, million years; Mt, million metric tons; %, percent; g/t, grams per metric ton; t, metric tons; n.d., no data. Contained Cu in metric tons is computed as tonnage (Mt × 1,000,000) × Cu grade (percent)]

Tract	Tract Name	Name	Age (Ma)	Tonnage (Mt)	Cu (%)	Mo (%)	Au (g/t)	Ag (g/t)	Contained Cu (t)	Contained Mo (t)	Contained Au (t)
142pCu8710	Yulong	Yulong	40.7	850	0.84	0.022	0.35	n.d.	7,140,000	187,000	298
		Zhanaga	38.5	99.5	0.32	0.03	0.03	n.d.	318,000	29,900	3
		Mangzhong	37.5	135	0.43	0.03	0.02	n.d.	581,000	40,500	3
		Duoxiasongduo	37.4	248	0.38	0.04	0.06	n.d.	942,000	99,200	15
		Malasongduo	36.0	338	0.45	0.014	0.06	n.d.	1,520,000	47,300	20
		Gegongnong	38.0	101	0.5	n.d.	0.37	2.65	505,000	n.d.	37
142pCu8711	Dali	Xifanping	32	64.3	0.28	n.d.	0.31	n.d.	180,000	n.d.	20
		Machanqing	35	62	0.5	0.078	0.35	n.d.	310,000	48,400	22
142pCu8712	Gangdese	Qulong	16.2	1,778	0.45	0.045	n.d.	3.9	8,000,000	800,000	nd
		Xietongmen/Newtongmen*	39#	1,085	0.30	n.d.	0.22	1.20	3,310,000	n.d.	241
		Jiama*	15.2	1,006	0.39	0.046	0.095	5.6	3,920,000	463,000	96
	total								26,700,000	1,720,000	755

* These two deposits are not completely explored, but they are included as deposits because their known resource is so large.
# Age is in dispute; may be Jurassic.

assessment reported in this document describes permissive areas for deposits of Cenozoic age within the Tibetan Plateau, a geographic region (fig. 1) that includes the Xizang (Tibet) Autonomous Region and parts of the Chinese provinces of Qinghai, Sichuan, and Yunnan.

This assessment report includes an overview of the results, and summary tables. Detailed descriptions of each tract are included in appendixes, which include estimates of numbers of undiscovered deposits, and probabilistic estimates of amounts of copper, molybdenum, gold, and silver that could be contained in undiscovered deposits for each permissive tract. A database and map prepared using a GIS (geographic information system) accompany the report, and include tract boundaries and a database of known porphyry copper deposits and significant prospects.

The assessment of undiscovered porphyry copper deposits on the Tibetan Plateau was conducted using the three-part form of mineral-resource assessment based on established mineral deposit models (Singer, 1993, 2007a,b; Singer and Berger, 2007; Singer and Menzie, 2010). In the three-part form of mineral resource assessment, geographic areas (permissive tracts) are delineated using geologic, geochemical, mineral occurrence, and geophysical data to identify areas with features typical of the type of deposit under consideration. In this study, three permissive tracts were defined: the Yulong permissive tract (142pCu8710) on the northeast margin of the Tibetan Plateau, the Dali permissive tract (142pCu8711) in the southeast corner, and the Gangdese permissive tract (142pCu8712) in south central part (fig. 1). Secondly, the amount of metal in undiscovered deposits is estimated using grade and tonnage models derived from information about known deposits. Probabilistic estimates of numbers of undiscovered deposits are consistent with the known deposits that define grade

and tonnage models (Singer, 2007a). And thirdly, estimates are made at different confidence levels using a variety of estimation strategies to express the degree of belief that some fixed but unknown number of deposits exists within the permissive tract. These estimates are measures of the favorability of the tract and of the estimator's uncertainty about what may exist (Singer, 2007a).

The Tibetan Plateau is an area of active mineral exploration, both by Chinese and international companies. Several projects, previously under development by Canadian and Australian companies, have recently reverted to full Chinese ownership. This report reflects the status of porphyry copper exploration projects known to the authors as of August 2011. The supply of copper is important for Chinese industry. Therefore, continued exploration for, and development of, porphyry copper deposits on the Tibetan Plateau is likely. Exploration in China, as elsewhere in the world, is presently focused on precious-metal deposits, due to current elevated metal prices, but porphyry copper systems may be associated with some precious-metal deposits and may be present in other parts of large exploration concessions under study for precious metals.

Terminology

The terminology used in this report follows the definitions used in the 1998 USGS assessment of undiscovered resources in the United States (U.S. Geological Survey National Mineral Resource Assessment Team, 2000). This terminology is intended to represent standard definitions that reflect general usage by the minerals industry and the resource assessment community.

• *Mineral deposit*—An occurrence of a valuable commodity or mineral that is of sufficient size and grade that it might, under the most favorable of circumstances, be considered to have potential for economic development.

• *Undiscovered mineral deposit*—A mineral deposit that is believed to exist or an incompletely explored mineral occurrence or prospect that could have sufficient size and grade to be classified as a deposit.

• *Mineral prospect*—A mineral concentration that is being actively examined to determine whether a mineral deposit exists.

• *Mineral occurrence*—A locality where a useful mineral or material is found.

• *Permissive tract*—The surface projection of a volume of rock whose geologic characteristics permit the existence of a mineral deposit of a specified type. The probability that deposits of the type being studied occur outside the boundary of the tract is negligible. In this report, the term is commonly abbreviated to "tract."

• *Resource*—A mineral concentration of sufficient size and grade, and in such form and amount that economic extraction of a commodity from the concentration is currently or potentially feasible.

• *Identified resources*—Resources whose location, grade, quality, and quantity are known or can be estimated from specific geologic evidence. For this assessment, identified resources are those in the porphyry copper deposits included in the grade and tonnage models used in the assessment (which can include measured, indicated, and inferred mineral resources at the lowest available cut-off grade). In addition, deposits that are not included in the models used for the assessment are considered to contain identified resources if they are characterized well enough to meet commonly used reporting guidelines.

• *S-type granite*—Granite in which geochemical and isotopic characteristics are primarily inherited through partial melting of a crustal sedimentary source.

Report Format

This report begins with a discussion of porphyry copper deposit models, both descriptive and grade-and-tonnage models. This is followed by a discussion of the tectonic history of the Tibetan Plateau and how that history has influenced the emplacement of magmatic rocks and the formation of porphyry copper deposits. The next section consists of comments about the nature and quality of the data that was gathered for the assessment, followed by a brief description of the exploration history of the area. Next, the processes used to delineate permissive tracts are described, and a brief description of the three permissive tracts is presented. The last section of the report describes the assessment process, including a description of how estimates of numbers of undiscovered deposits are made and a discussion of the assessment results and their significance. More detailed descriptions and assessment results for the three permissive tracts (Yulong, Dali, and Gangdese) evaluated in this report are presented in a standardized format in appendixes A, B, and C of this report. Tract boundaries and point locations of significant deposits and prospects are included in a geographic information system (GIS) in appendix D and appendix E identifies the members of the assessment team.

Political Boundaries

Political boundaries used in this report are, in accord with U.S. Government policy, the small-scale digital international boundaries (SSIB) provided by the U.S. Department of State (U.S. Department of State, 2009). In various parts of the world, some political boundaries are in dispute. The use of the boundaries certified by the U.S. Department of State does not imply that the U.S. Geological Survey advocates or has an interest in the outcome of any international boundary disputes.

Considerations for Users of this Assessment

Ideally, assessments are done on a recurring basis, at a variety of scales, because available data change over time. This GMRAP product represents a synthesis of current, readily available information, as of August, 2011. The assessment is based on the descriptive and grade-tonnage data contained in published mineral deposit models. Data in the grade and tonnage models represent the most reliable average grades available for each commodity of possible economic interest; the tonnages are based on the total of production, reserves, and resources at the lowest cutoff grade for which data were available when the model was constructed.

The economic viability of any mineral deposit depends on a wide variety of factors, many of which vary with time. This caveat applies to the deposits used to construct the grade-tonnage models, as well as to undiscovered deposits, so care must be exercised when using the results of this assessment to answer economic questions. If discovered, deposits may not be developed immediately or ever. Furthermore, the estimates in this assessment are of numbers of deposits that are likely to exist, not necessarily those likely to be discovered (Singer, 2007b). Prospects, revealed by past or current exploration efforts, may become deposits through further drilling and characterization. These probable deposits are treated here as undiscovered deposits, albeit ones with a high degree of certainty of existence.

The mineral industry explores for extensions of identified resources, as well as for undiscovered deposits. Extensions of identified resources are not estimated in this assessment, although they are commonly a substantial part of newly discovered copper resources each year.

This assessment considers the potential for both exposed deposits and concealed deposits within 1 kilometer (km) of the surface. Very high-grade deposits may be exploited at greater depths; however, it is not common. Exploration for, and possible exploitation of, these deeper deposits may be so expensive that they may not be discovered in the near term. If they are discovered, the cost to mine a deeply buried porphyry deposit may easily prohibit its development into a mine, given current or near-term metal prices and technology.

Permissive tracts are identified based on geology, irrespective of political boundaries. Therefore, tracts may cross country boundaries or include lands that already have either been developed for other uses, or have been withdrawn from mineral development as protected areas. The tracts are constructed at a scale of 1:1,000,000 and are not intended for use at larger scales.

Porphyry Copper Deposit Models

Porphyry copper deposits typically form in subduction-related, compressional tectonic settings, during active subduction of oceanic or continental crust (Sillitoe, 2010; John and others, 2010). These deposits are typically associated with shallowly emplaced calc-alkaline plutons. The Andes Range of South America is the classic province for continental arc magmatism (Kay and others, 1999; Richards and others, 2001). Magma associated with these deposits is typically hydrous, oxidized, and rich in sulfur, and has likely undergone complex processes of differentiation and evolution at the crust-mantle boundary (Richards, 2003; John and others, 2010). Island arcs in the southwest Pacific Ocean are the archetypes of island arc magmatism (Garwin and others, 2005). Magma associated with island arc porphyry copper deposits is similar to that associated with continental arcs, but diorite, quartz diorite, and other more mafic rocks are somewhat more abundant (Kesler and others, 1975).

In recent years, evidence has accumulated for the existence of a family of porphyry copper deposits that formed in a significantly different tectonic setting: extensional or transpressional regimes that form within cratons after active subduction has ceased. The porphyry copper deposits on the Tibetan Plateau are the classic and original examples of this family, but similar deposits are found in comparable settings in Mesozoic rocks on the eastern margin of the Yangtze (South China) craton, in Iran and Pakistan (Hou and others, 2011), and in other parts of the world. The geology and mineralization style characteristic of these deposits are broadly similar to those of classic porphyry copper deposits, however, the magmas that form them originated from as-yet poorly understood processes.

Richards (2009) presents a model based on the remelting of previously-subducted arc lithosphere. Such previously subducted lithosphere would contain small amounts of chalcophile and siderophile element-rich sulfide minerals, and would be a fertile source for hydrous, oxidized, gold-rich (but comparatively sulfur-poor) magmas. In his view, the remelting is triggered by postsubduction lithospheric thickening, lithospheric extension, or mantle lithosphere delamination (fig. 2).

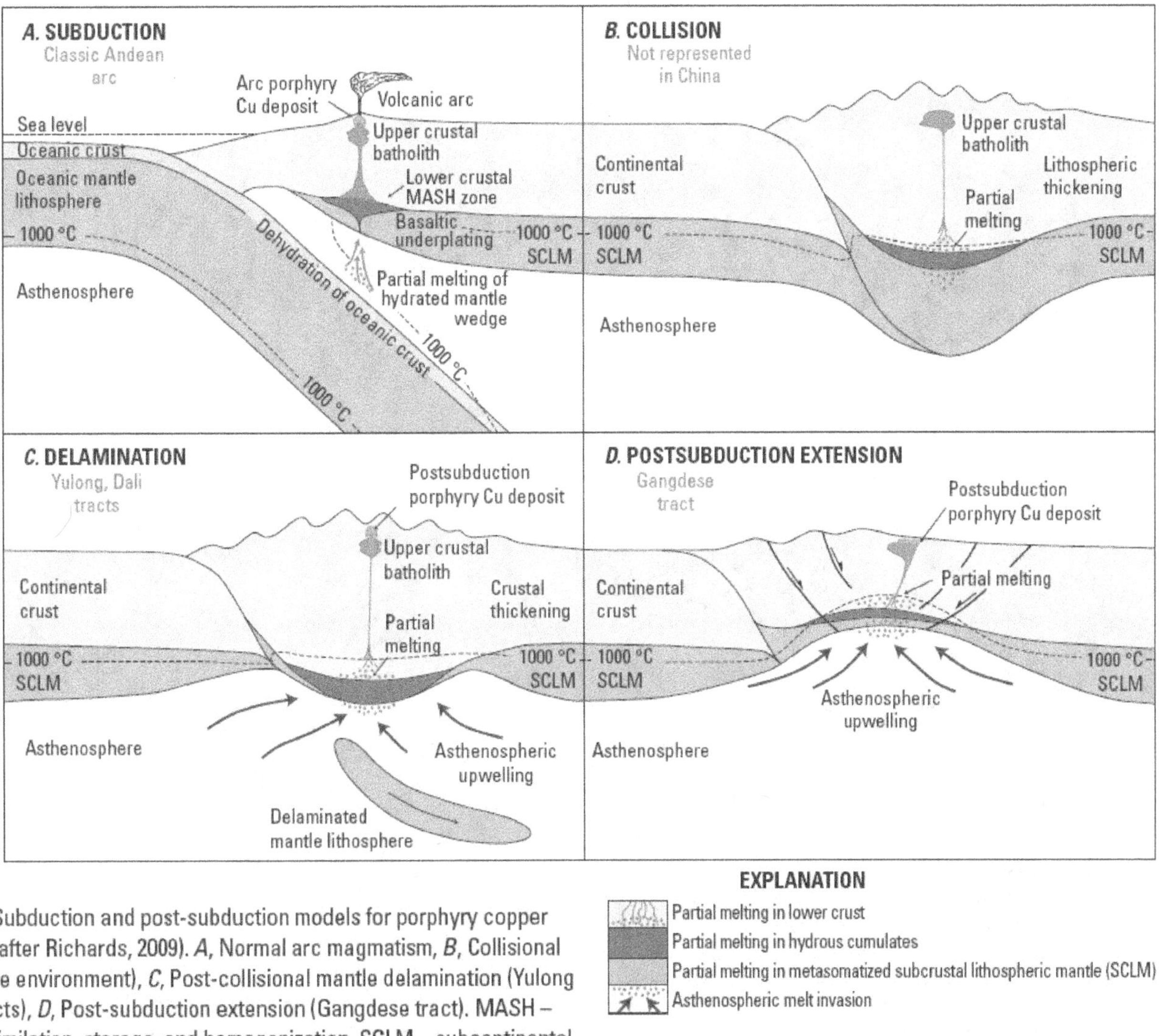

Figure 2. Subduction and post-subduction models for porphyry copper generation (after Richards, 2009). *A,* Normal arc magmatism, *B,* Collisional (compressive environment), *C,* Post-collisional mantle delamination (Yulong and Dali tracts), *D,* Post-subduction extension (Gangdese tract). MASH – melting, assimilation, storage, and homogenization. SCLM – subcontinental lithospheric mantle. In all cases, high Sr/Y magmas may be generated by residual or fractionating hornblende (±garnet, titanite).

EXPLANATION

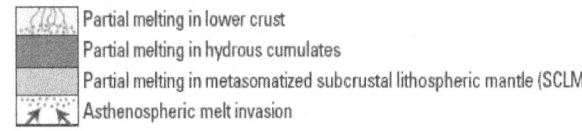

Partial melting in lower crust

Partial melting in hydrous cumulates

Partial melting in metasomatized subcrustal lithospheric mantle (SCLM)

Asthenospheric melt invasion

More recently, Hou and others (2011) have promulgated a model that involves partially melting thickened juvenile mafic lower crust or delaminated lower crust, including asthenospheric mantle components (fig. 3). The fertility of these magmas depends on the contribution of copper and gold from the mantle, thickened lower crust that has been metasomatized due to previous underplating, and the inclusion of crustal components (especially molybdenum) during crustal melting and magma ascent. They suggest that formation of these magmas is triggered by asthenospheric upwelling, lithospheric delamination, and/or large-scale translithospheric strike-slip faults or orogeny-transverse normal faults.

Both Richards (2009) and Hou and others (2011) stress that most magmas associated with post-subduction porphyry copper-gold deposits are mildly alkaline (shoshonitic), rather than calc-alkaline, and may form isolated complexes in contrast to volcanoplutonic arcs. At this time, there is no evidence that these deposits in post-subduction environments have different grade-tonnage relationships than other porphyry copper deposits and there is no basis to create a grade and tonnage model specific to these deposits.

Occurrence Models

Mineral deposit models used for this assessment include the porphyry copper models of Singer and others (2008), Cox (1986a,b), and John and others (2010). The recent review of salient features of porphyry copper deposits by Sillitoe (2010) is also pertinent. The global porphyry copper database of Singer and others (2008) contains tabulated descriptive information along with grade and tonnage data. Discussions of porphyry copper deposits related to the special post-subduction setting of the Tibetan deposits are given by Richards (2009) and Hou and others (2011).

Grade and Tonnage Models

The grade and tonnage models of Singer and others (2008) were used in this assessment of undiscovered resources in porphyry copper deposits on the Tibetan Plateau. In addition to the global porphyry copper-molybdenum-gold (Cu-Mo-Au)

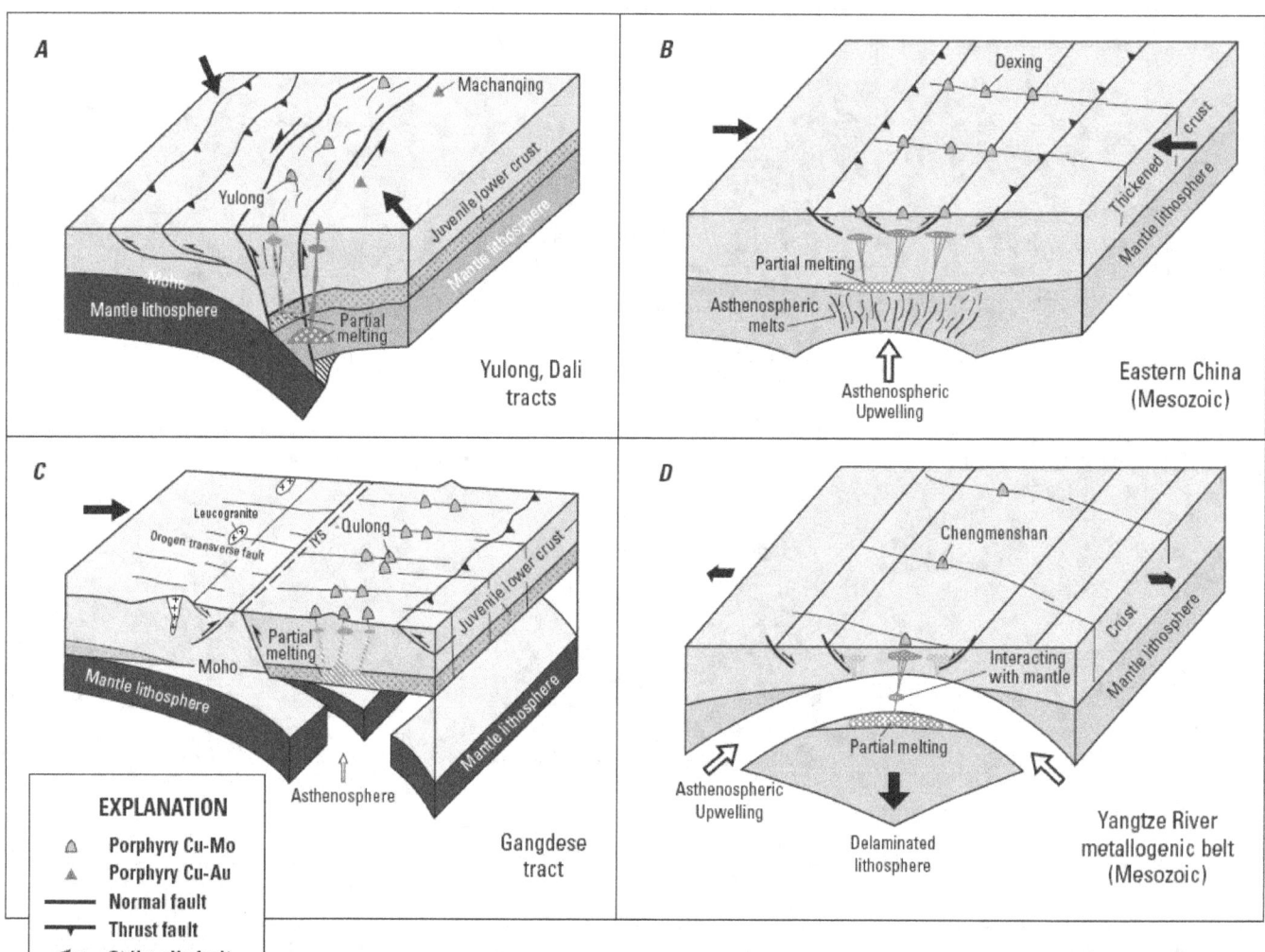

Figure 3. Models for porphyry copper deposits in non-arc settings (after Hou and others, 2011). *A,* Melting of lower crust triggered by translithospheric strike-slip faults in a late-collision, transpressional setting, *B,* Melting of thickened crust triggered by upwelling of asthenosphere in a post-collision, extensional setting, *C,* Melting of thickened, mafic lower crust, triggered by delamination of lithospheric root and upwelling of asthenosphere in an intracontinental, extensional setting, *D,* Melting of a delaminated lithospheric root and upwelling of asthenosphere in an anorogenic, extensional setting.

Table 2.   Statistical test results, porphyry copper assessment of the Tibetan Plateau.

[Pooled *t*-test results assuming equal variances; ANOVA tests used for tracts with a single deposit; $p>0.01$ indicates that the deposits in the tract are not significantly different from those in the model at the 1-percent level; $p<0.01$ indicates that the deposits in the tract are significantly different from those in the model at the 1-percent level and therefore, the tract fails the selected test and the model is inappropriate for the assessment. N_{known}, number of known deposits in the tract that are included in the grade and tonnage model; -, no data]

Coded_ID	Tract name	N_{known}	Model	p values					Model selected	Basis for selection
				Tons	Cu	Mo	Ag	Au		
142pCu8710	Yulong	6	Cu-Au-Mo	0.87	0.71	0.09	0.74	0.22	Cu-Au-Mo (general worldwide model)	*t*-test results
			Cu-Mo	0.31	0.84	0.83	0.54	0.0027		
			Cu-Au	0.89	0.77	<0.001	0.88	<0.001		
142pCu8711	Dali	2	Cu-Au-Mo	0.22	0.66	0.06	-	0.42	Cu-Au	*t*-test results and geologic context
			Cu-Mo	-	-	-	-	-		
			Cu-Au	0.24	0.63	0.002	-	0.64		

model that is based on data from 422 deposits, they identified two subtypes of porphyry copper deposit, each with distinct grade and tonnage models.

For each tract, if sufficient grade and tonnage data were available, the known deposits in the tract were tested against the global models using statistical tests (*t*-test or analysis of variance [ANOVA]) (table 2). For the Yulong tract, which contains six known deposits, these tests led to selection of the general (Cu-Mo-Au) model as the most appropriate. The Dali tract contains two deposits, each of which qualifies as a porphyry copper-gold deposit, and high gold grades at other prospects in that tract led to use of the gold-rich model for assessment of that tract. The Gangdese tract contains three known deposits, but each of them lacks crucial information on molybdenum or gold grades, precluding meaningful statistical tests, and the general model was used to assess that tract. The size of the known Tibetan deposits is comparable (fig. 4) to those in the worldwide model of Singer and others (2008).

Tectonic Setting

The porphyry copper deposits on the Tibetan Plateau that are described here formed during the Cenozoic Era, after the collision of the Indian continental plate with Eurasia, in a post-subduction setting. The tectono-magmatic history of the Tibetan Plateau has been summarized by Hou and Cook (2009). The plateau, which formed as a result of the collision of the Indian plate with Eurasia, is composed of four terranes; from north to south, they are the Songpan-Ganze, Qiangtang, Lhasa, and Tethyan Himalaya (Indian Plate) (Chu and others, 2006). These terranes are separated by three sutures: the Jinsa, the Bagong-Nujiang, and the Yarlung-Tsangpo (fig. 5). The Jinsa suture was formed during the closure of the Paleotethyan ocean in the Permian. The Bagong-Nujiang suture was formed by the closure of the Bagong (Tethyan) ocean in middle Jurassic time. The Yarlung-Tsangpo suture is the interface along which the Neotethyan ocean achieved final closure, as the Indian plate collided with Eurasia during Paleocene through Eocene time.

Each of these ocean closures terminated a continental-margin volcanic arc. The Permian and Middle Jurassic arcs are described in other chapters of this assessment. The late Mesozoic arc rocks north of the Yarlung-Tsangpo suture are described below.

The collision of the Indian Plate with Eurasia began in the west, in modern India and Pakistan, at about 65 Ma. As convergence progressed, the suture closure moved progressively eastward, and near the end of the Eocene, the amalgamation was complete. Previously, the strain of Indo-Asian convergence was accommodated primarily by crustal thickening and uplift

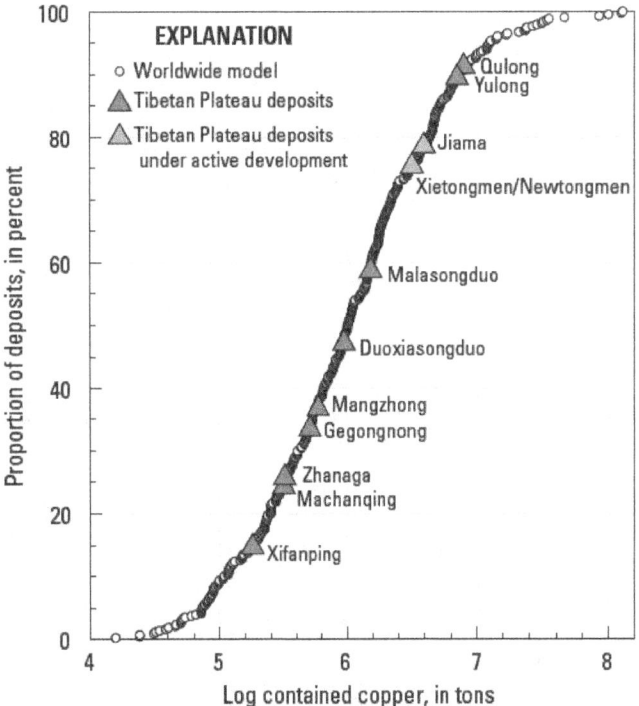

Figure 4.   Cumulative frequency plot showing tonnages of Tibetan Plateau porphyry copper deposits compared to worldwide deposits from the grade-tonnage model of Singer and others (2008).

of the Tibetan Plateau. Subsequently, the initiation of the left-lateral Sanjiang-Red River Fault Zone accommodated half or more of this strain by permitting the eastward extrusion of the Indochina terrane (Harrison and Yin, 2004). Most of the porphyry copper deposits in Tibet formed after the accretion of the Indian Plate to Eurasia.

Different authors have diverse opinions about the Cenozoic tectono-magmatic history of the region. Most of the controversy is about the chronologic details, which is not surprising as, in the last decade, dozens of new radiometric age determinations have been reported each year. For the purposes of this discussion, we subdivide the Cenozoic tectono-magmatic history into three periods (following Hou and Cook, 2009): 1) main-collisional (Paleocene and Eocene, about 65–41 Ma), 2) late-collisional (Eocene and Oligocene, about 41–26 Ma, and 3) post-collisional (Miocene and younger, about 26 Ma to the present).

Magmatic rocks associated with the main-collisional period range from I-type calc-alkaline rocks north of the Yarlung-Tsangpo suture (Gangdese batholith; Ji and others, 2009) that constitute the end stages of arc magmatism associated with the subduction of Tethyan oceanic crust to collision-related S-type muscovite-bearing granites, mostly found south of the Yarlung-Tsangpo suture where they intrude the Indian plate.

Late-collision stage (Eocene through Oligocene) magmatic rocks (primarily plutonic) are mostly high-K calc-alkaline and shoshonitic rocks emplaced between the Jinsa and Bagong-Nujiang sutures. Further south, along and east of the Jinsa suture and the Red River Fault Zone, most late-collisional rocks are alkaline, and include lamprophyres and carbonatites.

In the post-collision stage (Miocene and younger), magmatic rocks range from high-K calc-alkaline and shoshonitic rocks of the Gangdese porphyry belt to ultrapotassic rocks that are widespread on the Tibetan Plateau to leucogranites along the Yarlung-Tsangpo suture.

Igneous Provinces

Four major igneous provinces have formed on the Tibetan Plateau since the final accretion of the Indian Plate and the end of subduction (fig. 6): the Jinsa-Ailaoshan shoshonitic to alkaline igneous province, the Gangdese shoshonitic igneous

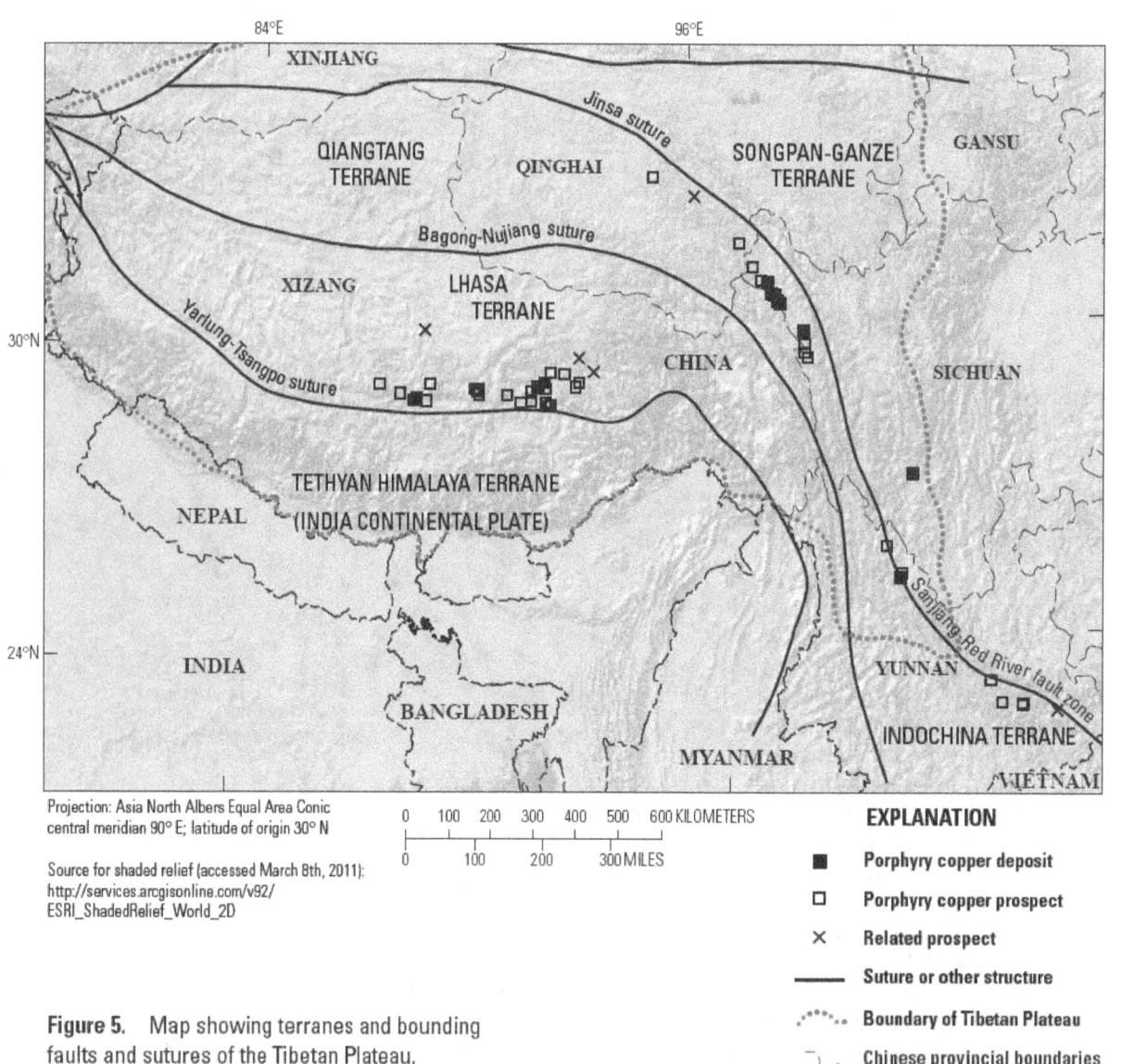

Figure 5.   Map showing terranes and bounding faults and sutures of the Tibetan Plateau.

province, the Tibetan potassic-ultrapotassic igneous province, and a peraluminous igneous province. The peraluminous province is located primarily south of the Yarlung-Tsangpo suture, within the Indian Plate. Since there are no porphyry or other copper-gold deposits associated with the peraluminous rocks, they are not discussed further.

Jinsa-Ailaoshan Shoshonitic to Alkaline Igneous Province

Cenozoic igneous rocks crop out along the entire length of the Jinsa suture and Sanjiang-Red River Fault Zone from northwestern Tibet into northern Vietnam (figs. 5, 6). Ages of the rocks range from Eocene (about 50 Ma) to recent. The rocks in the northwest part of the belt are commonly referred to as the Yulong belt, whereas those to the south are usually termed the Ailaoshan belt.

Eocene igneous rocks of the Yulong belt formed during continental-scale strike-slip faulting during the late-collision stage, primarily between about 46 and 35 Ma. They were emplaced into

the Qiangtang terrane, mostly between the Jinsa and Bagong-Nujiang sutures. The Qiangtang terrane is characterized by Precambrian crystalline rocks overlain by late Paleozoic shallow marine rocks and Mesozoic carbonate and clastic rocks. The crust in the Qiangtang terrane is 50 to 60 km in thickness—thinner than that of the Lhasa terrane to the south (70 to 80 km) (Hou and Cook, 2009). The emplacement of many of the plutons in the belt may be controlled by stepover extensional faults that formed between the major strike-slip faults in a transpressional regime (Hou and others, 2011).

Yulong Porphyry Belt

Igneous rocks in the Yulong porphyry belt are mostly intrusive, though a few volcanic remnants remain. They are best characterized as high-K calc-alkaline, although they have also been termed shoshonitic and adakitic by various authors. The following petrologic description is based primarily on the work of Jiang and others (2008), who made a comprehensive study of

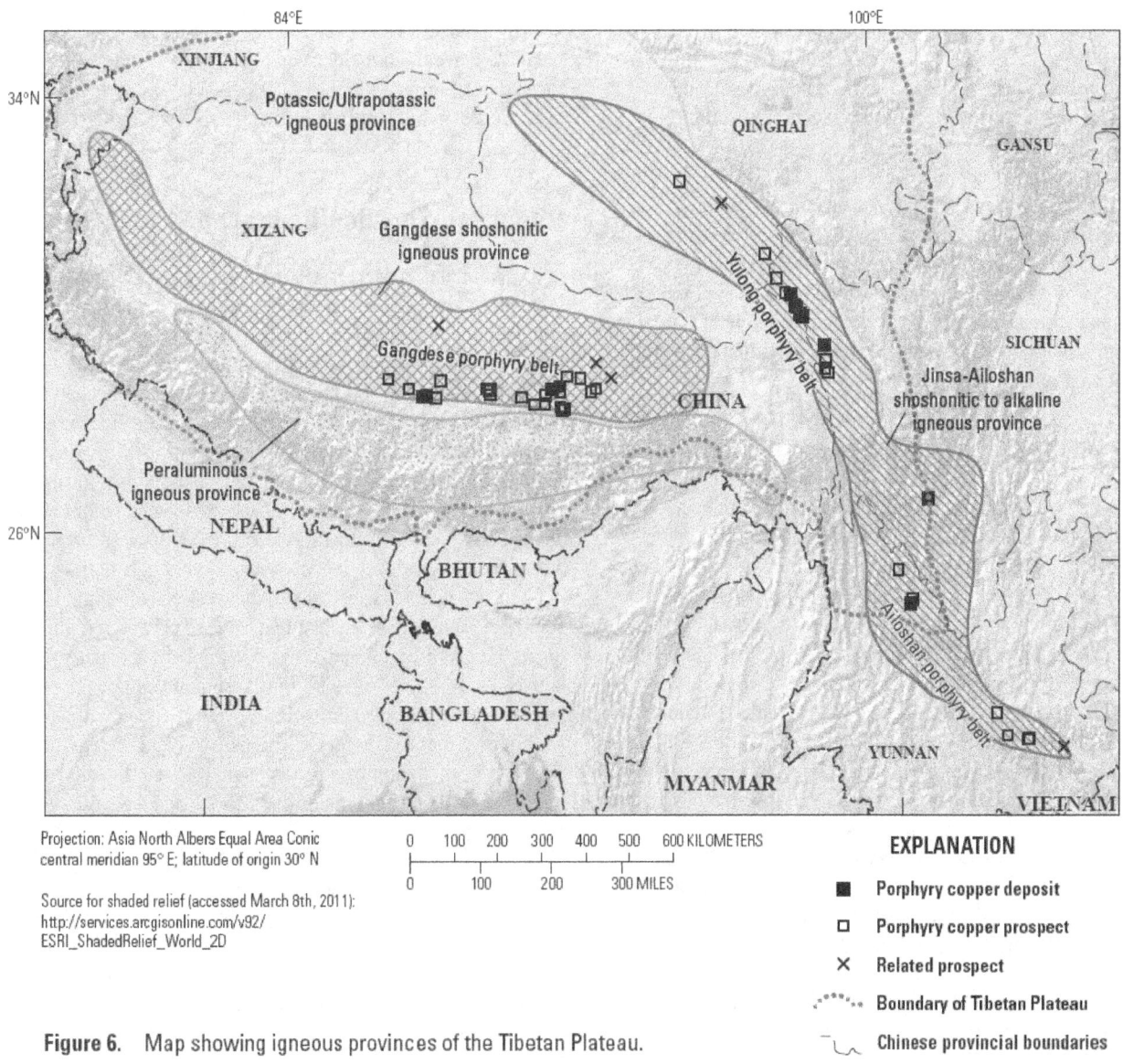

Figure 6.   Map showing igneous provinces of the Tibetan Plateau.

igneous rocks from much of the Yulong porphyry belt. Most of the ore-bearing porphyries are monzogranites and have silica contents between 67 and 72 percent. The Mamupu igneous center (fig. 1) in particular is more alkaline, and contains syenites with silica contents around 64 percent. High total alkali contents in most analyses indicate shoshonitic compositions. Yttrium contents are low, generally less than 20 ppm, and strontium is relatively high (500–2,000 ppm). Niobium is very low, mostly less than 15 ppm. Total rare-earth element (REE) contents are high, but rare-earth patterns are relatively gentle, with samarium/ytterbium (Sm/Yb) ratios of 5 to 8. Europium anomalies are generally absent. Isotopically, the analyses show moderate crustal contributions; $^{87}Sr/^{86}Sr$ ranges from 0.7055 to 0.7073, and ε_{Nd} values range from -2.0 to -4.1.

The magmas were strongly oxidized. The rocks are uniformly magnetite-bearing and Liang and others (2009) report that sulfate is the dominant sulfur species in early-formed fluid inclusions in magnetite and quartz. Mg numbers of biotites in these rocks range from 0.53 to 0.64 and the Fe^{3+}/Fe^{2+} ratios are mostly greater than one (Jiang and others, 2008). Additional evidence for oxidation is given by Liang and others (2006) who showed that ore-bearing porphyries in the Yulong porphyry belt have average Ce^{4+}/Ce^{3+} ratios in zircon of 200 to 300, in contrast to barren porphyries (ratios < 120) in the region.

Based on geochemical and isotopic data, Jiang and others (2008) have suggested that the source rocks for the Yulong belt magmas were probably garnet- and phlogopite-bearing pyroxenites, and that the melting occurred at depths near 100 km. They suggest that the melting of this metasomatized mantle was initiated by asthenospheric upwelling beneath the large trans-crustal strike-slip faults that define the tract. Initial magmatic temperatures were very high (>1200° C) and the magmas must have ascended rapidly. Jiang and others (2008) and Hou and others (2003, 2005) stress that plutonism is a response to the transtensional environment along major sutures that bound the tract.

Ailaoshan Porphyry Belt

Further south, most Cenozoic igneous rocks are decidedly more alkaline and are related to strike-slip faulting during the late-collision stage. The rocks range in age from about 40 Ma to about 26 Ma (Deng and others, 1998), slightly younger than the rocks in the Yulong belt to the north. They are emplaced along the Ailaoshan-Red River Fault Zone (the southern extension of the Jinsa suture), which forms the boundary between the Indochina plate and the South China craton, and which marks the suture between them (Wang and others, 2001; Guo and others, 2005). The Ailaoshan-Red River structure is a strike-slip fault zone that has accommodated much of the strain of the Indo-Asian collision since the Paleocene, and there are numerous subparallel strands of this fault. The igneous rocks also extend several hundred kilometers eastward onto the South China craton. In addition to the silicate rocks, a group of REE-bearing carbonatite complexes, with ages between about 40 and 10 Ma is found along the eastern margin of the province (Hou and others, 2009).

As in the Yulong porphyry belt to the north, the igneous rocks are mostly porphyritic intrusions, though a few volcanic rocks

are present. The majority of the plutons here are composed of syenite, with lesser numbers of granite and monzonite plutons, as well as numerous small bodies of mafic alkaline rock (Deng and others, 1998; Wu and others, 2005; Guo and others, 2005). Trace-element data for these rocks are scarce, but Deng and others (1998) summarize their data by reporting that the rocks are enriched in Rb, Sr, Ba, Zr, and Y. Analyses for a single unmineralized pluton (Wu and others, 2005) are consonant with this generalization. Chondrite-normalized rare-earth patterns are relatively flat, with minor or no Eu anomalies (see Peng and others, 1998, for patterns from the Machangqing (fig. 1) porphyry copper deposit). Isotopically, the rocks show moderate crustal contributions; most $^{87}Sr/^{86}Sr$ ratios range from about 0.705 to 0.708 and most ε_{Nd} values range from -1 to -5 (Deng and others, 1998). At least at Machangqing (fig. 1), magnetite is present in the early, high-temperature potassic alteration assemblages (Peng and others, 1998).

Based on trace-element and isotopic modeling, Guo and others (2005) present a compelling model for the origin of these alkaline rocks as products of the melting of metasomatized mantle at depths near 100 km. Hu and others (2004) studied He and Ar isotopes of samples from Machangqing and from some of the nearby alkaline-rock-related gold deposits and concluded that the plutons were mantle-derived. The trigger for the melting that formed alkaline rocks in the Ailaoshan belt was probably the movements on the large trans-crustal strike-slip faults that bound the area (Hou and others, 2005).

Gangdese Shoshonitic Igneous Province

Within the Lhasa terrane, in the southern part of the Tibetan Plateau, a suite of distinctive post-collisional plutons and small exposures of volcanic rock form a 1,500 km-long belt that is subparallel to the Yarlung-Tsangpo suture (fig. 5, 6). The report by Guo and others (2007) is the source of most of the petrologic data summarized here. The oldest rocks are Oligocene in age (about 26 Ma) and the youngest are Miocene (about 10 Ma); most of the plutons have ages between 18 and 12 Ma. Individual intrusions are small, most with areas < 100 km², and are located within north-south-trending grabens that formed during east-west extension. There are several dozen igneous centers, although all have probably not been catalogued, especially in the western part of the belt.

The rocks are mildly alkaline, and are primarily composed of quartz monzonite and monzonite. They are about equally divided between high-K calc-alkaline and shoshonitic compositions. The large-ion lithophile elements (Rb, K, Sr, Pb), along with U and Th, are highly enriched whereas the high field strength elements (Nb, Ta, Ti, HREE, Y) are strongly depleted. Rare-earth patterns show moderate slopes (La/Yb ratios of 20 to 50) and have minor or no Eu anomalies. The rocks show moderate crustal contributions; most $^{87}Sr/^{86}Sr$ ratios range from 0.7050 to 0.7075 and most ε_{Nd} values range from -6 to +5 (Hou and others, 2009).

Trace-element and isotopic modeling show that both melting of previously subducted oceanic crust and melting of mafic to intermediate metaigneous lower crustal rocks are permissive sources for these rocks. There is an emerging consensus that these rocks were formed from mantle-derived melts that have assimilated important amounts of lower crustal material, as well as some upper crustal material during ascent (Hou and others, 2009; Hou and others, 2011). This conclusion is based primarily on the position of these rocks in the $^{87}Sr/^{86}Sr$ vs. ε_{Nd} diagram. The cause of the melting is ascribed to upwelling asthenosphere, with the trigger for emplacement being the uplift and extension of the upper crust of the Tibetan Plateau. Perhaps the contemporaneous alkaline mantle-sourced melts described in the next section also provided heat for the formation of the shoshonites in the Gangdese belt (Guo and others, 2007).

Tibetan Potassic/Ultrapotassic Igneous Province

Post-collisional potassic and ultrapotassic igneous rocks, many of them volcanic, are distributed throughout the northern part of the Tibetan Plateau, and are described in a comprehensive review by Guo and others (2006). These rocks formed between about 45 Ma and the present, and are found in the Lhasa, Qiangtang, and Songpan-Ganze terranes, where they are closely associated with major thrust and strike-slip faults, and with pull-apart basins. They have relatively small volumes (mostly thin flows and less than 1,000 km^2 in extent), but more than 25 localities have been catalogued.

These rocks are notably alkaline, ranging from mildly shoshonitic to ultrapotassic; rock types include trachyte, trachyandesite, trachybasalt, phonolite, tephriphonolite, phonotephrite, and tephrite. Guo and others (2006) postulate that they formed by partial melting of enriched asthenospheric mantle, and were modified only slightly by crustal contamination, as indicated by extensive strontium, lead, and neodymium isotopic data. The trigger for this melting is interpreted to be prolonged northward underthrusting of Indian continental lithosphere beneath the Tibetan Plateau, resulting in the upwelling of hot asthenosphere. Magma likely ascended to the surface via deep transcrustal faults. There is no known porphyry copper style mineralization associated with these rocks, which formed in ways somewhat distinct from the other two largely contemporaneous igneous provinces (Gangdese and Jinsa-Ailaoshan).

The Adakite Issue

Adakite is a term that is commonly used in the Chinese literature to mean igneous rocks with trace-element compositions that suggest an origin by melting of metabasaltic crust at pressures high enough to stabilize garnet, probably at depths of as much as 100 km (Xiao and Clemens, 2007). The most diagnostic parameters are high Sr/Y (> 20) and steep chondrite-normalized REE patterns (La/Yb >20). Although the original definition (Defant and Drummond, 1990) was closely linked to origin through direct melting of a subducting oceanic slab, the term has been subsequently applied to rocks from other petrotectonic settings. Indeed, in a comprehensive review that documents the evolution of the meaning of the term, Castillo (2006) pointed out that there is no single model for the origin of the rocks defined by these geochemical criteria.

Most of the rocks associated with the Tibetan porphyry copper deposits have been classified as adakites and a correlation between porphyry copper deposits and adakitic compositions has been noted in many parts of the world (Thiéblemont and others, 1997; Mungall, 2002). Direct melting of the slab, however, has been shown to be unsatisfactory as a unique factor in the genesis of porphyry copper deposits (Richards and Kerrich, 2007). Although we embrace the idea that plutons that give rise to porphyry copper deposits commonly have high Sr/Y and La/Yb, we avoid the use of the term adakite whenever possible in this assessment.

Assessment Data

Geologic Maps

Geologic maps at a variety of scales were used during the assessment. The conceptual basis for the generalized versions of the tracts is the discussion by Hou and Cook (2009) outlining the magmatic history of the region. As a basis for tract delineation, we used unpublished digital versions of geological maps of the Chinese provinces published as part of a collection of Geologic Memoirs by the Chinese Ministry of Geology and Mineral Resources from 1984 through 1993. The resulting digital geologic map does not always reflect the most recent radiometric age determinations or petrologic studies of the rocks in the tract; in many cases, ages of the igneous rocks are not accurately known. Many of the small plutons that host porphyry copper deposits in the region are too small to be depicted on that map and we digitized the location of additional plutons based on available small-scale schematic maps (Guo and others, 2006, 2007; Qu and others, 2007; Hou and others, 2009).

In addition, we consulted the digital geologic map of China based on the 1:2,500,000 scale map by the China Geological Survey (2004a). Although this map is at a smaller scale than those in the geologic memoirs, it incorporates significant new petrologic and radiometric age data gathered in the 1990s for the new maps of the Tibetan Plateau (Wang and others, 2004; Zhai, 2004).

Mineral Occurrence Data

A global database of porphyry copper deposits and prospects published by Singer and others (2008) was supplemented with other global and regional mineral occurrence databases, including that of the Geological Survey of Canada (Natural Resources Canada, 2010; Kirkham and Dunne, 2000). In addition, commercially available databases (InfoMine, Intierra, Metals Economic Group), technical reports, company websites, and geologic literature were consulted. The U.S. Geological Survey Mineral Resources Data System (MRDS), an online searchable database, also includes information on mines, prospects, and mineral occurrences worldwide.

Sites were classified as deposits (grade and tonnage well-delineated) or prospects (incompletely characterized with respect to grade and tonnage) on the basis of recent published literature. The deposit-type classification of some sites is ambiguous due to insufficient information. Deposits and prospects that could be classified with certainty as porphyry copper or porphyry-copper-related are included in the database for this report (appendix D).

Distributions of gold placers, copper and copper-gold skarns, and epithermal precious-metal deposits, as well as unclassified copper and gold occurrences, were considered during the assessment but generally are not included in the database. Some skarns were included if it seemed likely that an associated porphyry system could be plausibly inferred.

Geochemical Data

Stream-sediment geochemistry has been very important for mineral exploration in China. Begun in 1978, the Regional Geochemistry-National Reconnaissance project has now covered more than 6 million km^2 of the territory of China, and has been directly responsible for the discovery of hundreds of mineral deposits, including several porphyry copper deposits (Xie and others, 2008). Although the data themselves are not available to the general public, the China Geological Survey has made numerous national maps for specified elements available on the internet.

Maps (China Geological Survey, 2010) that show the distribution of copper (fig. 7) and bismuth were used to help refine the tracts defined in this study.

ASTER Data

Remote sensing data is also helpful in determining the extent of mineralized regions because hydrothermally altered areas associated with porphyry copper deposits can be identified. It is particularly useful in an arid region with only sparse vegetation like the Tibetan Plateau. A reconnaissance study of selected areas on the Tibetan Plateau was conducted using methods described by Mars and Rowan (2006). Preliminary results of this study indicate that large areas in the western part of the Gangdese tract exhibit abundant argillic and phyllic alteration, which increases the likelihood that the western part of the tract contains undiscovered porphyry copper deposits. Two illustrative examples of the ASTER data are shown in figure 8.

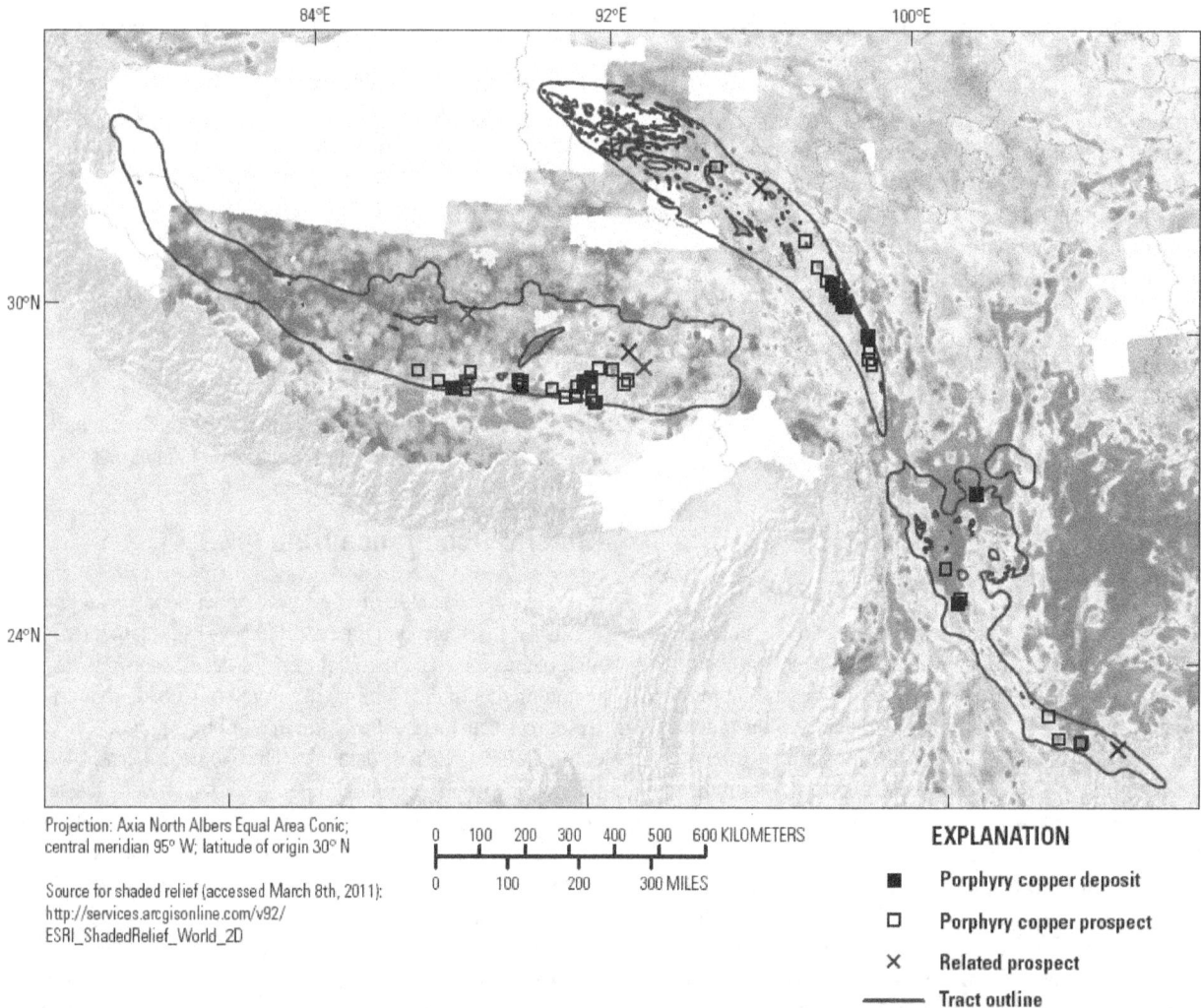

Figure 7. Map showing grid generated from stream-sediment geochemical data for copper in western China, along with permissive tract boundaries. After China Geological Survey (2010). Isolated copper anomalies may be related to porphyry deposits. Large continuous anomalies like those in the southeast quarter of the map area are likely to be related to bulk rock geochemistry (in this case, Cu-rich flood basalts). Values represented on the map range from 4 ppm (dark blue) through 30–35 ppm (yellow) to >150 ppm (dark red).

Other Data

Global aeromagnetic data covers most of Southeast Asia (National Geophysical Data Center, 2009). However, the data are of limited use in tracing the subsurface extent of magmatic arcs as a result of coarse flight-line spacing relative to the complex geology of the region. The published 1:5,000,000-scale aeromagnetic map of China (China Geological Survey, 2004b) is similarly of limited use.

Exploration History

In many parts of the world, porphyry copper exploration has been cyclic in response to changing global economic trends and the evolution of local infrastructure development. Exploration for porphyry copper deposits on the Tibetan Plateau is in its initial cycle. The porphyry copper deposit model was not well-known in China until the 1960s, when scientific and industrial activity was renewed after a long period of warfare and internal turmoil. Access to the region was also severely limited, due to limited infrastructure. Subsequently, basic geologic mapping and detailed geochemical and geophysical surveys have been completed, resulting in the discovery of numerous porphyry copper deposits and prospects (Wang and others, 2004; Xie and others, 2008). A few international companies based outside of China have operated in the region since about 1990, but most of the exploration activity has been conducted by Chinese companies and is not well documented in the English language literature.

The Assessment Process

A preliminary workshop attended by USGS and CGS scientists was held in Kunming, China, in September of 2005. At this meeting, preliminary tracts were delineated using non-digital methods. The CGS published the outlines of these tracts along with an associated quantitative resource assessment based on them (Yan and others, 2007). Meanwhile, assessment technology continued to evolve, and in 2009, the USGS decided to apply the standardized procedures adopted by the GMRAP, and updated the assessment. Preliminary versions of this assessment were presented to the Coordinating Committee for Geoscience Programmes in East and Southeast Asia (CCOP) workshop in Busan, South Korea, in the spring of 2010. The assessment was further refined after internal USGS review.

Three-Part Assessment

This assessment was conducted using methods, procedures, and models that support what have come to be known as three-part assessments. The three parts that are integrated to create the assessment are (1) delineation of permissive tracts, according to the type of mineral deposits permitted by geology, (2) estimation of the amount of metal in typical deposits by using grade-tonnage models, and (3) probabilistic estimation of the number of undiscovered deposits by subjective methods (Singer, 2007a; Singer and Menzie, 2010).

A permissive tract for porphyry copper deposits is delineated as a geographic area that includes intrusive and volcanic rocks

Figure 8. Map showing hydrothermally altered areas identified by ASTER. *A*, Nimu project area, eastern Gangdese belt; *B*, Poorly explored area in western part of Gangdese tract. Red pixels represent phyllic alteration, yellow pixels represent argillic alteration. Areas like those in *B* are common in southwestern Tibet.

of specified ranges of composition and age that are part of a magmatic arc. These arcs have been traditionally related to convergent plate margins, but the Cenozoic magmatic arcs related to porphyry copper deposits on the Tibetan Plateau formed after subduction ceased. The tract generally is bounded by the outline of the magmatic arc as depicted at the scale of the maps available for tract delineation and may include areas covered by younger or structurally overlying materials that are less than 1 km thick. For these Cenozoic tracts on the Tibetan Plateau, many of the igneous rocks closely associated with porphyry copper formation are not depicted on available geologic maps. In a number of cases, we used conceptual (tectonic) features to subjectively define tract boundaries, rather than relying directly on digital geologic maps.

Frequency distributions of pre-mining tonnages and average grades of thoroughly explored deposits are used as models for grades and tonnages of undiscovered deposits (Singer, 1993). Models are constructed from average grades and tonnages (including both measured and inferred resources) based on the total production, reserves, and resources at the lowest possible cutoff grade, as described by Singer and others (2008).

Numbers of undiscovered deposits at various quantiles (degrees of belief) are estimated by an assessment team of experts using a variety of strategies, such as counting the number and ranking the favorability of significant prospects, and comparing the spatial density of known deposits and expected undiscovered deposits to that of known deposits in similar, well-explored regions (Singer, 2007b). Probable amounts of undiscovered resources are then estimated by combining estimates of numbers of undiscovered deposits with grade and tonnage models, using a Monte Carlo simulation process (Root and others, 1992; Bawiec and Spanski, 2012; Duval, 2012).

Tract Delineation

The geology-based strategy that is commonly used for porphyry copper tract delineation within GMRAP is described here. Digital geologic data were processed in a GIS using ArcMap software, as follows:

Regional-scale maps and geologic literature were used to identify the fundamental units for tract delineation—magmatic arcs or belts of igneous rocks of a given age range.

Digital geologic maps were then used to select map units to define preliminary tracts permissive for porphyry copper deposits. Igneous map units were subdivided by age groups and classified as permissive or non-permissive based on lithology. Permissive rocks include calc-alkaline and alkaline plutonic and volcanic rocks. Non-permissive rocks include, for example, ultramafic assemblages, ophiolites, highly evolved granites, peraluminous granites, and pillow basalts.

Typically, a 10-, 15-, or 20-km buffer was then applied to plutonic rock polygons and a 2-km buffer to volcanic rock polygons; this generally expanded the area of the tract to include all porphyry copper deposits and significant associated prospects. The buffer accounts for uncertainties in the cartographic position of mapped boundaries, as well as possible unexposed or unmapped permissive rocks.

After buffering, available data on mineral deposits and occurrences, locations of dated igneous rock samples, and geophysical and geochemical information were examined to identify previously unrecognized evidence of unmapped permissive rocks or hydrothermal systems.

An aggregation and smoothing routine was applied to the resulting polygons, and the tracts were edited by hand in accord with post-mineral fault boundaries. In some cases, more detailed geologic maps were used to resolve tract boundary issues or available schematic map illustrations from the literature were incorporated to augment the existing digital maps.

Areas where post-mineral volcanic centers, depositional basins, and other forms of cover judged to exceed 1 km in thickness were excluded from the tracts. Intrusions younger than the designated tract age were also excluded.

Because many of the intrusions that define the tracts on the Tibetan Plateau are so small that they are not depicted on the available digital geologic maps, and because the igneous belts are believed to be controlled by deep trans-crustal faults, some of the major tract boundaries were subjectively delineated to include the entire area judged to be permissive.

Permissive Tracts for Porphyry Copper Deposits on the Tibetan Plateau

Based on the geologic data evaluated, three porphyry copper permissive tracts were delineated on the Tibetan Plateau (fig. 9). Table 3 contains comparative information about each of the tracts. Brief summaries of the tracts are included here, but the detailed rationale for tract delineation is in appendixes A, B, and C.

Yulong Tract

The Yulong tract (142pCu8710), with an area of about 112,000 km², is defined by a curvilinear belt of Eocene and early Oligocene (46–35 Ma) intrusions that are mostly shoshonitic and intermediate to felsic in composition and are part of the Jinsa-Ailaoshan igneous province. They formed in a transpressional environment closely related to the two sutures (Jinsa and Bagong-Nujiang) that bound the tract; they may be localized by stepover extensional faults that formed between the two sutures. The tract includes six known deposits (Yulong, Zhanaga, Mangzhong, Duoxiasongduo, Malasongduo, and Gegongnong; table 1) and at least six prospects (appendix A).

Dali Tract

The Dali tract (142pCu8711), with an area of about 97,000 km², is defined by a group of late Eocene and Oligocene (40–26 Ma) porphyritic, distinctly alkaline intrusions that are also part of the Jinsa-Ailaoshan magmatic province. The intrusions are both felsic and mafic, and are accompanied by sparse volcanic rocks that were emplaced along and to the east of the Ailaoshan-Red River shear zone and strike-slip fault. The tract includes two known deposits, Xifanping (32 Ma; table 1) and Machanqing

Table 3. Permissive tracts for porphyry copper deposits on the Tibetan Plateau.

Appendix	Coded_Id	Tract Name	Countries	Area (sq. km)	Geologic feature assessed
A	142pCu8710	Yulong	China	112,470	A curvilinear belt of Eocene igneous rocks formed in an extensional, post-subduction environment in southwest China during the collision between India and Asia
B	142pCu8711	Dali	China and Vietnam	96,670	An assemblage of Eocene and Oligocene igneous rocks formed in an extensional, post-subduction environment in southwest China during the collision between India and Asia
C	142pCu8712	Gangdese	China	239,860	A belt of Miocene igneous rocks formed in an extensional, post-subduction environment in southwest China after the collision between India and Asia

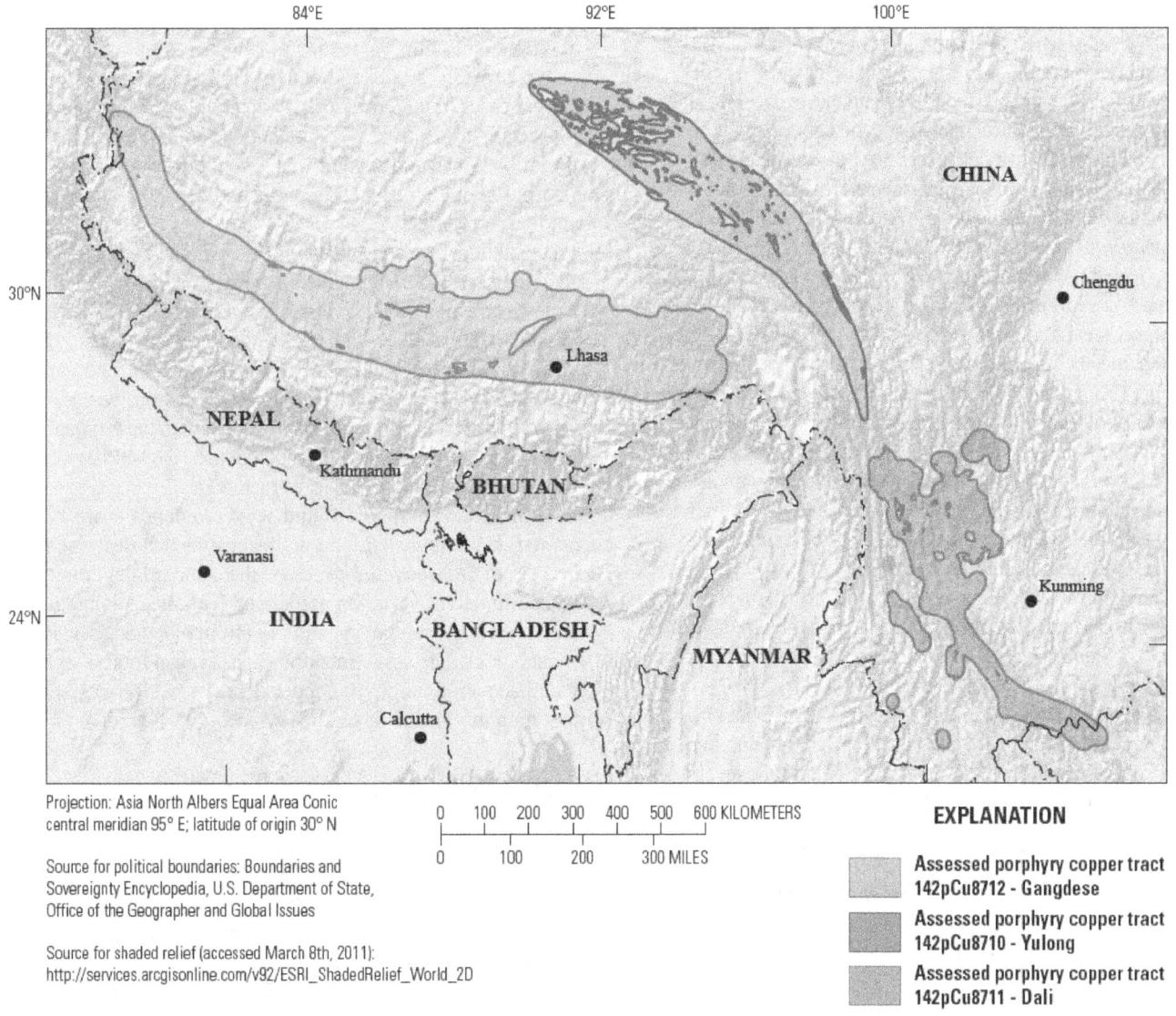

Figure 9. Map showing permissive tracts for porphyry copper deposits on the Tibetan Plateau.

(34–35 Ma; table 1), and as many as seven prospects in various stages of exploration and development (appendix B).

Gangdese Tract

The Gangdese tract (142pCu8712), with an area of about 240,000 km², is defined by a narrow 1,500-km-long belt of Miocene (22–12 Ma) high-K calc-alkaline to shoshonitic porphyryitic intrusions that formed in an east-west extensional environment and that are part of the Gangdese igneous province. The tract includes three deposits (Qulong, Xietongmen/Newtongmen, and Jiama; table 1) and more than 20 additional prospects in various stages of exploration and development (appendix C). Several of these prospects have been at least partially explored by drilling. Most discoveries have been in the eastern part of the tract, but discoveries are likely in the western, poorly explored part.

Estimating Numbers of Undiscovered Deposits

The assessment team estimated numbers of undiscovered deposits in each tract at various probabilities (degrees of belief). Strategies for estimation included counting the number and ranking the favorability of significant prospects, and comparing the spatial density of known deposits and expected undiscovered deposits to that of known deposits in similar, well-explored regions (Singer, 2007b).

Assessment team members evaluated the available data and made individual, subjective estimates of the numbers of undiscovered porphyry copper deposits by using expert judgment. Estimates are expressed in terms of different levels of certainty. Estimators are asked for the least number of deposits of a given type that they believe could be present at three specified levels of certainty (90 percent, 50 percent, and 10 percent). For example, on the basis of all available data, a team member might estimate that there was a 90-percent chance of 1 or more, a 50-percent chance of 5 or more, and a 10-percent chance of 10 or more undiscovered deposits in a permissive tract. The differences between individual estimates were discussed and evaluated before a single team estimate was agreed upon for each tract.

The estimates were converted to an expected (mean) number of deposits and standard deviation using an algorithm developed by Root and others (1992). This algorithm can be described by the following general equations (Singer and Menzie, 2005), which are used to calculate a mean expected number of deposits (λ) and a standard deviation (s_X) based on estimates of numbers of undiscovered deposits predicted at specified quantile levels[5] (N_{90} = 90 percent level, N_{50} = 50 percent level, etc.):

$$\lambda = 0.233\,N_{90} + 0.4\,N_{50} + 0.225\,N_{10} + 0.045\,N_{05} + 0.04\,N_{01} \qquad (1)$$

$$s_X = 0.121 - 0.237\,N_{90} - 0.093\,N_{50} + 0.183\,N_{10} + 0.073\,N_{05} + 0.123\,N_{01} \qquad (2)$$

For the example given above (N_{90} = 1; N_{50} = 5; N_{10} = 10), λ = 5.2 and s_X = 3.2.

---

[5]To use the equation in cases where three non-zero quantiles (90-50-10) are estimated, use the N_{10} values for N_{05} and N_{01}; where four quantiles (90-50-10) are estimated use the N_{05} value N_{01}.

Another useful parameter for reporting uncertainty associated with an estimate is the coefficient of variation (C_v), defined as:

$$C_v = s_X / \lambda \qquad (3)$$

The coefficient of variation is often reported as percent relative variation ($100 \times C_v$).

The final set of undiscovered deposit estimates reflects both the uncertainty in what may exist and the favorability of the tract (Singer, 1993). The estimates are combined with appropriate grade and tonnage models in a Monte Carlo simulation using the EMINERS computer program (Bawiec and Spanski, 2012; Duval, 2012), based on the original Mark3 computer program described by Root and others (1992), to provide a probabilistic estimate of amounts of resources that could be associated with undiscovered deposits.

The rationales for individual tract estimates are discussed in the appendixes. Recent literature, company websites, and technical reports for exploration projects were examined for descriptions of geology, mineralogy, deposit type, rock alteration, and sampling results to evaluate the likelihood that a prospect is associated with a porphyry copper system. In some cases, the number of significant porphyry copper prospects within a tract were counted as an important factor in estimation. Particular weight was given to prospects described as porphyry copper-related in published literature and recent exploration reports.

In addition, we considered the distribution of reported copper and gold occurrences of unknown type and placer gold workings. The level of exploration was also a factor in making estimates. In less well-explored areas, and areas with poor documentation of mineral occurrences, we were unable to use such methods, and the spread in estimates and relatively high coefficients of variations associated reflect the uncertainty associated with the estimates. We also considered the fact that much of the Tibetan Plateau is extremely remote, and lacks infrastructure.

Final team estimates of undiscovered deposits are summarized in table 4, along with statistics that describe mean numbers of undiscovered deposits, the standard deviation and coefficient of variation associated with the estimate, the number of known deposits, and the implied deposit density for each tract. The assessment predicts a mean total of about 39 undiscovered porphyry copper deposits in all tracts, many more than the 11 that have already been discovered.

Probabilistic Assessment Results

Probable amounts of undiscovered resources are estimated by combining estimates of numbers of undiscovered deposits with grade and tonnage models by using a Monte Carlo simulation (Root and others, 1992; Bawiec and Spanski, 2012; Duval, 2012). Frequency distributions of tonnages and average grades of thoroughly-explored deposits are used as models for grades and tonnages of undiscovered deposits (Singer, 1993). Data for the models include the average grade of each metal or commodity of possible economic interest and

Table 4. Estimates of numbers of undiscovered porphyry copper deposits on the Tibetan Plateau.

[N_{xx}, estimated number of deposits associated with the xxth percentile; N_{und}, expected number of undiscovered deposits; s, standard deviation; C_v%, coefficient of variance; N_{known}, number of known deposits in the tract that are included in the grade and tonnage model; N_{total}, total of expected number of deposits plus known deposits; area, area of permissive tract in square kilometers; -, no estimate made; deposit density reported as the total number of deposits per km²; N_{und}, s, and C_v% are calculated using a regression equation (Singer and Menzie, 2005)]

Appendix	Coded_Id	Tract Name	Consensus undiscovered deposit estimates					Summary statistics					Tract Area (km²)	Deposit density (N_{total}/km²)	Deposit density (N_{total}/100k km²)
			N_{90}	N_{50}	N_{10}	N_{05}	N_{01}	N_{und}	s	C_v%	N_{known}	N_{total}			
A	142pCu8710	Yulong	3	6	18	18	18	8.5	5.7	67	6	14.5	112,470	0.00013	12.9
B	142pCu8711	Dali	2	6	18	18	18	8.3	5.9	72	2	10.3	96,670	0.00011	10.6
C	142pCu8712	Gangdese	9	13	50	50	50	22.3	15.7	71	3	25.3	239,860	0.00011	10.5

Table 5. Summary of simulations of undiscovered resources in porphyry copper deposits and comparison with identified copper and gold resources in porphyry copper deposits within each permissive tract on the Tibetan Plateau.

[t, metric tons; Mt, million metric tons, n.a., not applicable (only means are additive)]

Appendix	Coded_Id	Tract Name	Known resources		Mean undiscovered copper resources (t)	Median undiscovered copper resources (t)	Mean undiscovered gold resources (t)	Median undiscovered gold resources (t)	Mean		Rock (Mt)
			copper (t)	gold (t)					Undiscovered molybdenum resources (t)	Undiscovered silver resources (t)	
A	142pCu8710	Yulong	11,000,000	376	32,000,000	20,000,000	820	470	910,000	11,000	6,600
B	142pCu8711	Dali	490,000	42	26,000,000	15,000,000	1,900	1,200	150,000	8,600	5,200
C	142pCu8712	Gangdese	15,200,000	337	87,000,000	61,000,000	2,200	1,500	2,400,000	28,000	18,000
Total			26,700,000	755	145,000,000	n.a.	4,920	n.a.	3,460,000	55,000	29,800

the associated tonnage based on the total production, reserves, and resources at the lowest possible cutoff grade, as described by Singer and others (2008).

The Monte Carlo simulation yields estimates for the mean and median copper and gold contained in undiscovered deposits (table 5). Identified resources in the table refer to metal contained in well-delineated porphyry copper deposits only; the resource data are based on total production, plus measured, indicated, and inferred reserves and resources at the lowest cutoff grade reported. Identified resources may include substantial amounts of metal that have already been produced.

All three permissive tracts contain identified resources, although those in the Dali tract are considerably less than in the Yulong or Gangdese tracts. All of the tracts also contain porphyry copper systems that have been partially explored, but for which no reliable grade and tonnage estimates are yet available. Resources in deposits like these that have not been comprehensively drilled out are not included in the data for identified resources. These deposits were considered to be significant prospects with a high probability of representing deposits like those in the grade and tonnage models. An example is the Gangjiang deposit, where a near-surface oxide resource of 47,000,000 t of ore has been identified, but deep drilling of the sulfide part of the deposit has just begun.

Simulation results are reported at selected quantile levels, along with the mean expected amount of metal, the probability of the mean, and the probability of no metal. The amount of metal reported at each quantile represents the least amount of metal expected. The quantile estimates are linked to each tract simulation and, therefore, should not be added. Mean estimates, however, can be added to obtain total amounts of metal and mineralized rock that can be compared between tracts.

Discussion

This probabilistic assessment of undiscovered resources in undiscovered porphyry copper deposits on the Tibetan Plateau indicates that significant amounts of additional resources may be present (table 5). The mean estimate of undiscovered copper resources in the study area (about 145,000,000 t) is nearly 6 times the amount of copper present in identified porphyry resources (about 27,000,000 t). This is entirely plausible for an area that is in the early stage of exploration. In 2006, China's reserve base was reported to be 30,700,000 t of copper and the identified copper resources were 70,500,000 t, contained in more than 1,000 identified mines, many of them small (Li, 2008). At the same time, annual consumption was nearly 5,000,000 t and growing rapidly. Thus, the undiscovered resources on the Tibetan Plateau may play an important role in meeting China's copper supply needs in the short and medium term.

However, a significant part of these resources, if they are present, may be inaccessible or uneconomic. Results should be interpreted with due caution, as no economic filters have been applied to these results to evaluate what portion of the estimated undiscovered resources might be economic under various conditions. For each tract, identified resources are compared with mean and median estimates of undiscovered copper resources in figure 10.

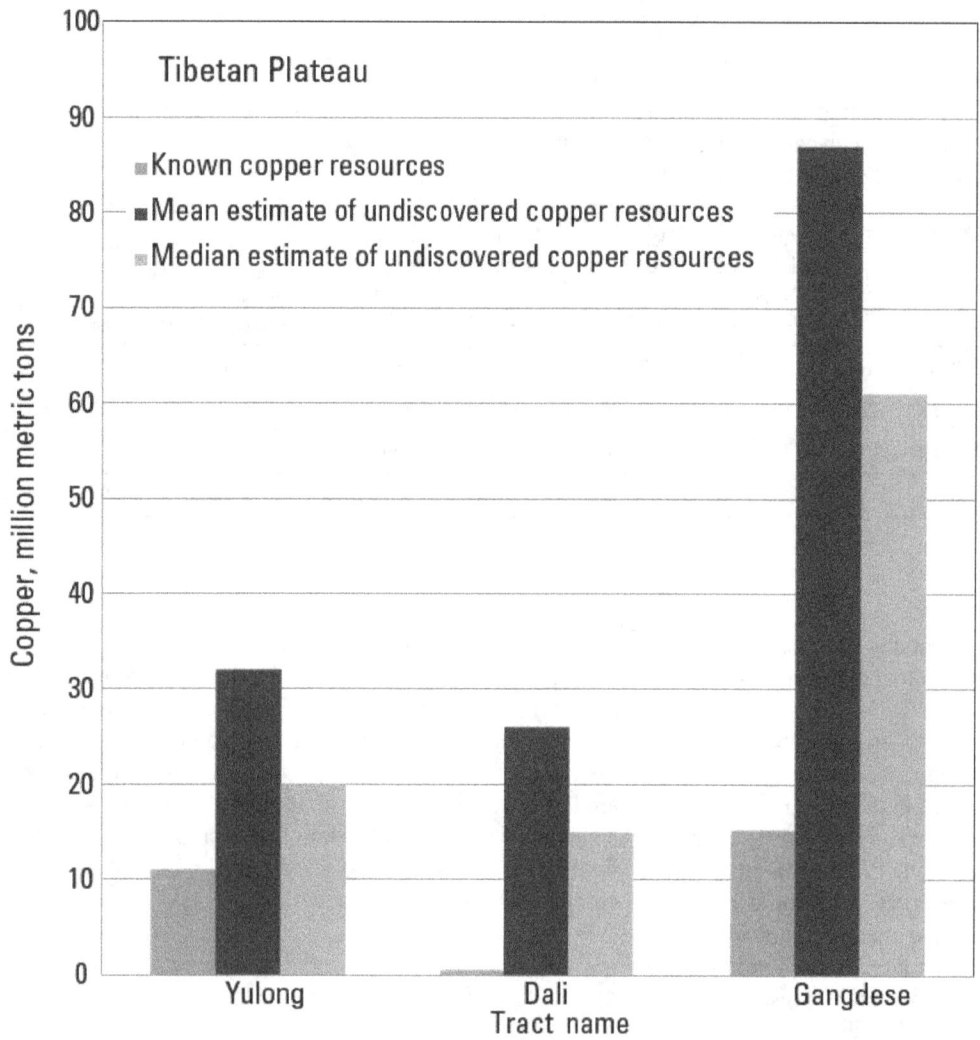

Figure 10.   Chart showing identified and undiscovered copper resources for permissive tracts on the Tibetan Plateau.

References Cited

Bawiec, W.J., and Spanski, G.T., 2012, Quick-start guide for version 3.0 of EMINERS—Economic Mineral Resource Simulator: U.S. Geological Survey Open-File Report 2009–1057, 26 p., accessed June 30, 2012, at http://pubs.usgs.gov/of/2009/1057. (This report supplements USGS OFR 2004–1344.)

Castillo, P.N., 2006, An overview of adakite petrogenesis: Chinese Science Bulletin, v. 51, p. 257–268.

China Geological Survey, 2004a, Geological map of the People's Republic of China: SinoMaps Press, 8 sheets, scale 1:2,500,000.

China Geological Survey, 2004b, Magnetic anomaly map of the People's Republic of China and its adjacent waters: Geological Publishing House, Beijing, scale 1:5,000,000.

Chu, Meifei, Chung, Sunlin, Song, Biao, Liu, Dunyi, O'Reilley, S.Y., Pearson, N.J., Ji, Jianqing, and Wen, Daren, 2006, Zircon U-Pb and Hf isotope constraints on the Mesozoic tectonics and crustal evolution of southern Tibet: Geology, v. 34, p. 745–748.

Cox, D.P., 1986a, Descriptive model of porphyry Cu (Model 17), *in* Cox, D.P., and Singer, D.A., eds., 1986, Mineral deposit models: U.S. Geological Survey Bulletin 1693, p. 76. (Also available at http://pubs.usgs.gov/bul/b1693/.)

Cox, D.P., 1986b, Descriptive model of porphyry Cu-Au, *in* Cox, D.P., and Singer, D.A., eds., 1986, Mineral deposit models: U.S. Geological Survey Bulletin 1693, p. 110. (Also available at http://pubs.usgs.gov/bul/b1693/.)

Defant, M.J. and Drummond, M.S., 1990, Derivation of some modern arc magmas by melting of young subducted lithosphere: Nature, v. 347, p. 662–665.

Deng, Wanming, Huang, Xuan, and Zhong, Dalai, 1998, Alkali-rich porphyry and its relation with intraplate deformation of north part of Jinsha River belt in western Yunnan, China: Science in China, series D, v. 41, p. 297–305.

Dunne, K.P.E, and Kirkham, R.V. (comps.), 2003, World distribution of porphyry, porphyry-related skarn, and bulk-mineable epithermal deposits: Geological Survey of Canada, unpublished, accessed February 17, 2010 at http://gdr.nrcan.gc.ca/minres/metadata_e.php?id=6.)

Duval, J.S., 2012, Version 3.0 of EMINERS—Economic Mineral Resource Simulator: U.S. Geological Survey Open-File Report 2004–1344, accessed June 30, 2012, at http://pubs.usgs.gov/of/2004/1344.

Garwin, S., Hall, R., and Watanabe, Y., 2005, Tectonic setting, geology, and gold and copper mineralization in Cenozoic magmatic arcs of southeast Asia and the west Pacific, *in* Hedenquist, T.W., Thompson, J.F.H., Goldfarb, R.J., and Richards, J.P., eds., One hundredth anniversary volume 1905-2005: Littleton, Colorado, Society of Economic Geologists, p. 891–930.

Gu, X.X., Tang, J.X., Wang, C.S., Chen, J.P., and He, B.B., 2003, Himalayan magmatism and porphyry copper-molybdenum mineralization in the Yulong ore belt, East Tibet: Mineralogy and Petrology, v. 78, p. 1–20.

Guo, Zhengfu, Hertogen, Jan, Liu, Jiaqi, Pasteels, Paul, Boven, Ariel, Punzalan, Lea, He, Huaiyu, Luo, Xiangjun, and Zhang, Wenhua, 2005, Potassic magmatism in western Sichuan and Yunnan Provinces, SE Tibet, China—Petrological and geochemical constraints on petrogenesis: Journal of Petrology, v. 46, p. 33–78.

Guo, Zhengfu, Wilson, Marjorie, and Liu, Jiaqi, 2007, Post-collisional adakites in south Tibet—Products of partial melting of subduction-modified lower crust: Lithos, v. 96, p. 205–244.

Guo, Zhengfu, Wilson, Marjorie, Liu, Jiaqi, and Mao, Qian, 2006, Post-collisional, potassic and ultrapotassic magmatism of the northern Tibetan Plateau—Constraints on characteristics of the mantle source, geodynamic setting and uplift mechanisms: Journal of Petrology, v. 47, p. 1177–1220.

Harrison, T.M. and Yin, An, 2004, Timing and processes of Himalyan and Tibetan Uplift: Himalayan Journal of Sciences, v. 2, (special issue), p. 152–153.

Hou, Zengqian and Cook, Nigel J., 2009, Metallogenesis of the Tibetan collisional orogen—A review and introduction to the special issue: Ore Geology Reviews, v. 36, p. 2–24.

Hou, Zengqian, Ma, Hongwen, Zaw, Khin, Zhang, Yuquan, Wang, Mingjie, Wang, Zeng, Pan, Guitang, and Tang, Renli, 2003, The Himalayan Yulong porphyry copper belt—Product of large-scale strike-slip faulting in eastern Tibet: Economic Geology, v. 98, p. 125–145.

Hou, Zengqian, Yang, Zhiming, Qu, Xiaoming, Meng, Xiangjin, Li, Zhenqing, Beaudoin, G., Rui, Zongyao, Gao, Yongfeng, and Zaw, Khin, 2009, The Miocene Gangdese porphyry copper belt generated during post-collisional extension in the Tibetan Orogen: Ore Geology Reviews, v. 36, p. 25–51.

Hou, Zengqian, Zhang, Hongrui, Pan, Xiaofei, and Yang, Zhiming, 2011, Porphyry (Cu-Mo-Au) deposits related to melting of thickened mafic lower crust—Examples from the eastern Tethyan metallogenic domain: Ore Geology Reviews, v. 39, p. 21–45.

Hou, Zenqian, Zhong, Dalai, Deng, Wanming, and Zaw, Khin, 2005, A tectonic model for porphyry copper-molybdenum-gold deposits in the eastern Indo-Asian collision zone, *in* Porter, T.M., ed., Super porphyry copper and gold deposits—A global perspective: Adelaide, PGC Publishing, v. 2, p. 423–440.

Hu, Ruizhong, Burnard, P.G., Bi, Xianwu, Zhou, Meifu, Pen, Jianteng, Su, Wenchao, and Wu, Kaixing, 2004, Helium and argon isotope geochemistry of alkaline intrusion-associated gold and copper deposits along the Red River–Jinshajiang fault belt, SW China: Chemical Geology, v. 203, p. 305–317.

Ji, Wei Qiang, Wu, Fu Yuan, Liu, Chuan Zhou, and Chung, Sun Lin, 2009, Geochronology and petrogenesis of granitic rocks in Gangdese batholith, southern Tibet: Science in China, Series D: Earth Sciences, v. 52, p. 1240–1261.

Jiang, Yaohui, Jiang, Shaoyong, Dai, Baozhang, and Ling, Hongfei, 2008, Origin of ore-bearing porphyries in the Yulong porphyry copper deposit, East Tibet: Beijing Geological Publishing House, 122 p.

John, D.A., Ayuso, R.A., Barton, M.D., Blakely, R.J., Bodnar, R.J., Dilles, J.H., Gray, Floyd, Graybeal, F.T., Mars, J.C., McPhee, D.K., Seal, R.R., Taylor, R.D., and Vikre, P.G., 2010, Porphyry copper deposit model, chap. B of Mineral deposit models for resource assessment: U.S. Geological Survey Scientific Investigations Report 2010-5070-B, 169 p., accessed September 8, 2010, at http://pubs.usgs.gov/sir/2010/5070/b/.

Kay, S.M., Mpodozis, C., and Coira, B, 1999, Neogene magmatism, tectonism, and mineral deposits of the central Andes (22° to 33° S. latitude), *in* Skinner, B.J., ed., Geology and ore deposits of the Central Andes: Society of Economic Geologists, Special Publication 7, p. 27–59.

Kesler, S.E., Jones, L.M., and Walker, R.L., 1975, Intrusive rocks associated with porphyry copper mineralization in island arc areas: Economic Geology, v. 70, p. 515–526.

Kirkham, R.V., and Dunne, K.P.E., 2000, World distribution of porphyry, porphyry-associated skarn, and bulk-tonnage epithermal deposits and occurrences: Geological Survey of Canada Open File 3792a, 26 p.

Li, Yusheng, 2008, Chinese copper market and industry—Current status and prospect: presentation at Joint CNIA/Study Groups' Seminar, Metals in China, 32nd Meeting of the International Copper Study Group, not paginated, accessed August 9, 2011, at http://www.icsg.org/index.php?option=com_docman&task=cat_view&gid=27&Itemid=62.

Liang, Huaying, Campbell, I.H., Allen, C., Sun, Weidong, Liu, Congqiang, Yu, Hengxiang, Xie, Wingwen, Zhang, Yuqiang, 2006, Zircon Ce^{4+}/Ce^{3+} ratios and ages for Yulong ore-bearing porphyries in eastern Tibet: Mineralium Deposita, v. 41, p. 152–159.

Liang, Huaying, Sun, Weidong, Su, Wenchao, and Zartman, Robert E., 2009, Porphyry copper-gold mineralization at Yulong, China, promoted by decreasing redox potential during magnetite alteration: Economic Geology, v. 104, p. 587–596.

Mars, J.C., and Rowan, L.C., 2006, Regional mapping of phyllic- and argillic-altered rocks in the Zagros magmatic arc, Iran, using Advanced Spaceborne Thermal Emission and Reflection Radiometer (ASTER) data and logical operator algorithms: Geosphere, v. 2, p. 161–186.

Mungall, J.E., 2002, Roasting the mantle—Slab melting and the genesis of major Au and Au-rich Cu deposits: Geology, v. 30, p. 915–918.

National Geological Archives of China, 2010a, Copper geochemical map: accessed on July 17, 2011, at http://www.ngac.cn/Gallery_New/Default.aspx?tab=last&type=image&node=13&id=966.

National Geological Archives of China, 2010b, Bismuth geochemical map: accessed on July 17, 2011, at http://www.ngac.cn/Gallery_New/Default.aspx?tab=last&type=image&node=9&id=966.

National Geophysical Data Center, 2009, EMAG2— Earth Magnetic Anomaly Grid (2-arc-minute resolution): National Oceanic and Atmospheric Administration, National Geophysical Data Center, Boulder, Colorado, accessed July 29, 2010, at http://www.geomag.us/models/emag2.html.

Natural Resources Canada, 2010, World minerals geoscience database: Natural Resources Canada, Ottawa, accessed February 19, 2010, at http://gsc nrcan.gc.ca/wmgdb/index_e.php.

Peng, Z., Watanabe, M., Hoshino, K., Sueoka, S., Yano, T., and Nishido, H., 1998, The Machangqing copper-molybdenum deposits, Yunnan, China—An example of Himalayan porphyry-hosted Cu-Mo mineralization: Mineralogy and Petrology, v. 63, p. 95–117.

Qu, Xiaoming, Hou, Zengqian, Zaw, Khin, and Li, Youguo, 2007, Characteristics and genesis of Gangdese porphyry copper deposits in the southern Tibetan Plateau—Preliminary geochemical and geochronological results: Ore Geology Reviews, v. 31, p. 205–223.

Richards, J.P., 2003, Tectono-magmatic precursors for porphyry (Cu-Mo-Au) deposit formation: Economic Geology, v. 98, p. 1515–1533.

Richards, J.P., 2009, Postsubduction porphyry Cu-Au and epithermal Au deposits—Products of remelting subduction-modified lithosphere: Geology, v. 37, no. 3, p. 247–250.

Richards, J.P., Boyce, A.J., and Pringle, M.S., 2001, Geologic evolution of the Escondida area, northern Chile—A model for spatial and temporal location of porphyry Cu mineralization: Economic Geology, v. 96, p. 271–306.

Richards, J.P. and Kerrich, Robert, 2007, Adakite-like rocks—Their diverse origins and questionable role in metallogenesis: Economic Geology, v. 102, p. 537–576.

Root, D.H., Menzie, W.D., and Scott, W.A., 1992, Computer Monte Carlo simulation in quantitative resource estimation: Natural Resources Research, v. 1, no. 2, p. 125–138.

Sillitoe, R.H., 2010, Porphyry copper systems: Economic Geology, v. 105, p. 3–41.

Singer, D.A., 1993, Basic concepts in three-part quantitative assessments of undiscovered mineral resources: Nonrenewable Resources, v. 2, no. 2, p. 69–81.

Singer, D.A., 2007a, Short course introduction to quantitative mineral resource assessments: U.S. Geological Survey Open-File Report 2007-1434, accessed May 15, 2009, at http://pubs.usgs.gov/of/2007/1434/.

Singer, D.A., 2007b, Estimating amounts of undiscovered resources, in Briskey, J.A., and Schulz, K.J., eds., Proceedings for a workshop on deposit modeling, mineral resource assessment, and their role in sustainable development, 31st International Geological Congress, Rio de Janeiro, Brazil, August 18-19, 2000: U.S. Geological Survey Circular 1294, p. 79–84. (Also available online at http://pubs.usgs.gov/circ/2007/1294/.)

Singer, D.A., 2010, Progress in integrated quantitative mineral resource assessments: Ore Geology Reviews, v. 38, p. 242–250.

Singer, D.A., and Berger, V.I., 2007, Deposit models and their application in mineral resource assessments, in Briskey, J.A., and Schulz, K.J., eds., Proceedings for a workshop on deposit modeling, mineral resources assessment, and their role in sustainable development, 31st International Geological Congress, Rio de Janeiro, Brazil, August 18-19, 2000: U.S. Geological Survey Circular 1294, p. 71–78. (Also available online at http://pubs.usgs.gov/circ/2007/1294/.)

Singer, D.A., Berger, V.I., and Moring, B.C., 2008, Porphyry copper deposits of the world: U.S. Geological Survey Open-File Report 2008–1155, 45 p., accessed August 10, 2009, at http://pubs.usgs.gov/of/2008/1155/.

Singer, D.A., and Menzie, W.D., 2010, Quantitative mineral resource assessments—An integrated approach: New York, Oxford University Press, 219 p.

Thiéblemont, D., Stein, G., and Lescuyer, J.-L., 1997, Gisements épithermaux et porphyriques—La connexion adakite: Académie de Sciences Paris, Comptes Rendus, v. 325, p. 103–109. [In French with English abstract.]

U.S. Department of State, 2009, Small-scale digital international land boundaries (SSIB)—Lines, edition 10, and polygons, beta edition 1, in Boundaries and sovereignty encyclopedia (B.A.S.E.): U.S. Department of State, Office of the Geographer and Global Issues.

U.S. Geological Survey National Mineral Resource Assessment Team, 2000, 1998 assessment of deposits of gold, silver, copper, lead, and zinc in the United States: U.S. Geological Survey Circular 1178, 21 p.

Wang, Jianghai, Yin, An, Harrison, T.M., Grove, Marty, Zhang, Yuquan, and Xie, Guanghong, 2001, A tectonic model for Cenozoic igneous activities in the eastern Indo-Asian collision zone: Earth and Planetary Science Letters, v. 188, p. 123–133.

Wang, Liquan, Zhu, Dicheng, and Pan, Guitang, 2004, Introduction to recent advances in regional geological mapping (1:250,000) and new results from southern Qinghai-Tibet Plateau: Himalayan Journal of Sciences, v. 2, (special issue), p. 195.

Wu, Kaixing, Hu, Ruizhong, Bi, Xianwu, Peng, Jiantang, Zhan, Xinzhi, and Chen, Long, 2005, Island-arc geochemical signatures of Cenozoic alkali-rich intrusive rocks from western Yunnan and their implication: Chinese Journal of Geochemistry, v. 24, p. 361–369.

Xiao, L. and Clemens, J.D., 2007, Origin of potassic (C-type) adakite magmas—Experimental and field constraints: Lithos, v. 95, p. 399–414.

Xie, Xuejing, Wang, Xueqiu, Zhang, Qin, Zhou, Guohua, Cheng, Hangxin, Liu, Dawen, Cheng, Zhizhong, and Xu, Shanfa, 2008, Multi-scale geochemical mapping in China: Geochemistry—Exploration, Environment, Analysis, v. 8, p. 333–341.

Yan Guangsheng, Qiu Ruizhao, Lian Changyun, Nokleberg, Warren J., Cao Li, Chen Xiufa, Mao Jingwen, Xiao Keyan, Li Jinyi, Xiao Qinghui, Zhou Su, Wang Mingyan, Liu Dawen, Yuan Chunhua, Han Jiuxi, Wang Liangliang, Chen Zhen, Chen Yuming, Xie Guiqing, and Ding Jianhua, 2007, Quantitative assessment of the resource potential of porphyry copper systems in China: Earth Science Frontiers, v. 14, p. 27–41.

Yang, Zhiming, Hou, Zengqian, White, Noel C., Chang, Zhaoshan, Li, Zhenqing, and Song, Yucai, 2009, Geology of the post-collisional porphyry copper–molybdenum deposit at Qulong, Tibet: Ore Geology Reviews, v. 36, p. 133–159.

Zhai, Gangyi, 2004, New significant advances of regional geological survey in the blank regions of Qinghai-Xizang Plateau: Himalayan Journal of Sciences, v. 2, (special issue), p. 136–137.

Appendixes A–E

Appendix A. Porphyry Copper Assessment for Tract 142pCu8710, Yulong—China

By Steve Ludington[1], Jane M. Hammarstrom[2], Gilpin R. Robinson, Jr.[2], and Robert J. Miller[1], based on contributions of Yan Guangsheng[3], Peng Qiuming[3], Lian Changyun[3], and Dennis Cox[1]

Deposit Type Assessed: Porphyry Copper

Deposit type: Porphyry copper
Descriptive model: Porphyry copper (Cox, 1986; John and others, 2010)
Grade and tonnage model: General porphyry copper (Singer and others, 2008)
Table A1 summarizes selected assessment results.

Table A1. Summary of selected resource assessment results for tract 142pCu8710, Yulong—China.

[km, kilometers; km², square kilometers; t, metric tons]

Date of assessment	Assessment depth (km)	Tract area (km²)	Known copper resources (t)	Mean estimate of undiscovered copper resources (t)	Median estimate of undiscovered copper resources (t)
2010	1	112,470	11,000,000	32,000,000	20,000,000

Location

The tract extends for about 1,100 kilometers (km), from southern Qinghai Province in China, through easternmost Xizang (Tibet) and a few kilometers into northernmost Yunnan (fig. A1). Much of the tract is quite narrow, but parts are as much as 160 km wide. The tract is entirely within the Tibetan Plateau, and most of it is at altitudes exceeding 4,000 meters (m). Much of the southern part of the tract is coincident with the Ningjing Shan range, between the Mekong and Yangtze Rivers.

Geologic Feature Assessed

A curvilinear belt of Eocene igneous rocks that formed in a transtensional, post-subduction environment in southwest China during the collision between India and Asia.

[1]U.S. Geological Survey, Menlo Park, California, United States.

[2]U.S. Geological Survey, Reston, Virginia, United States.

[3]China Geological Survey, Beijing, China.

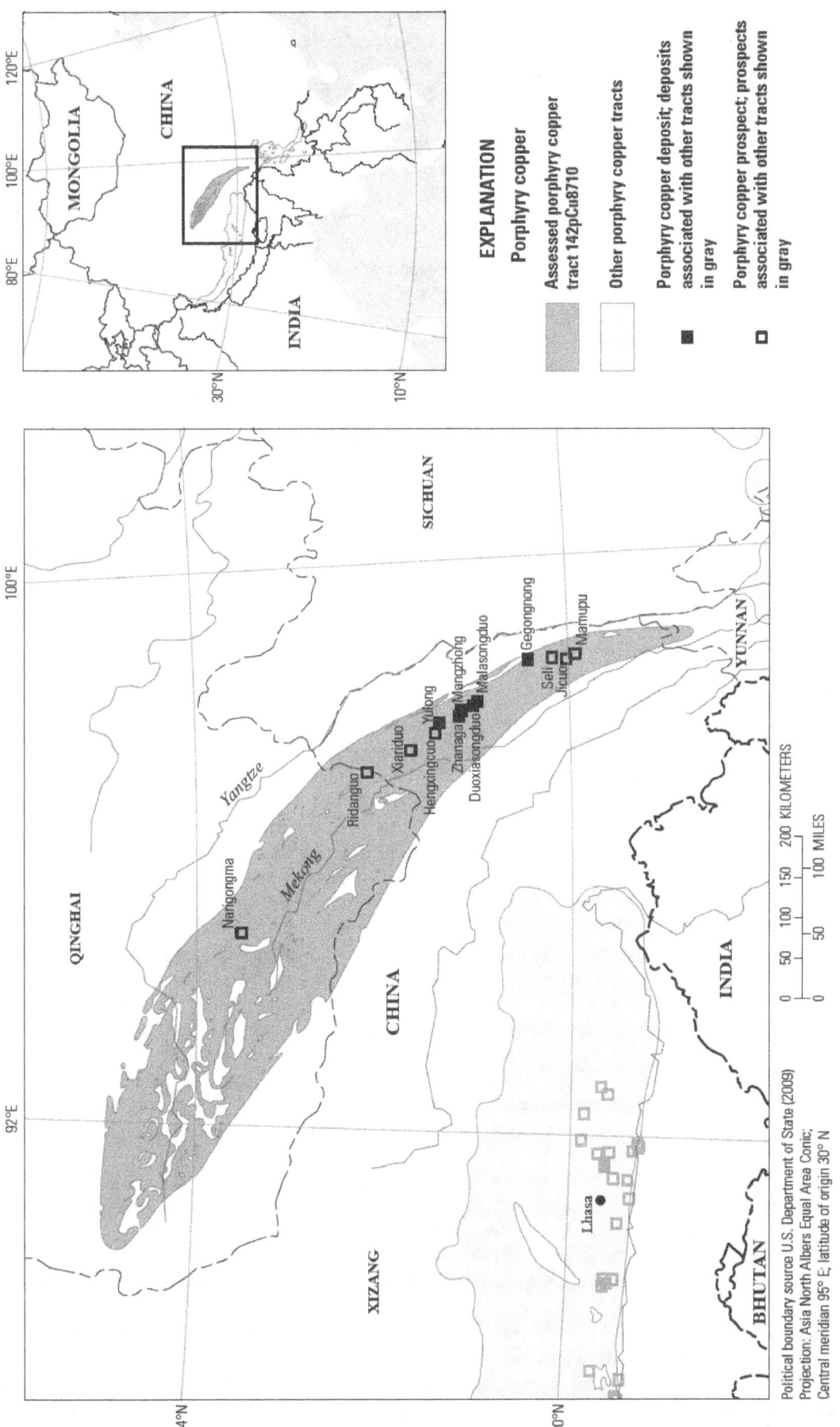

Figure A1.   Map showing tract location, known porphyry copper deposits, and significant porphyry copper prospects for tract 142pCu8710, Yulong—China.

Delineation of the Permissive Tract

Geologic Criteria

The igneous rocks that define the Yulong tract formed during continental-scale strike-slip faulting that accompanied the late-collision stage of the accretion of India to Asia. They are emplaced into the Qiangtang terrane, between the Jinsa and Bangong-Nujiang sutures (fig. 5). The faults that bound the magmatic belt (Chesuo and Tuoba) are strike-slip faults that have accommodated the strain associated with the Indo-Asian collision since the Paleocene and numerous other strike-slip faults parallel the two main faults (Jiang and others, 2006). Emplacement of many of the plutons in the belt may have been controlled by stepover extensional faults that formed between these strike-slip faults in a transpressional regime (Hou and others, 2007b, 2011). The six known porphyry copper deposits and seven prospects in the tract were formed between about 46 and 35 million years (Ma) ago. They are concentrated in the southeastern, better-explored, part of the tract (fig. A1).

The igneous rocks are mostly intrusive, though a few volcanic remnants crop out. Most of them are best characterized as high-K calc-alkaline (Jiang and others, 2008), although they have also been termed shoshonitic and adakitic by various authors. They are uniformly magnetite-bearing (Liang and others, 2009a). The source rocks that were melted at depths near 100 km were probably garnet- and phlogopite-bearing pyroxenite.

As a basis for tract delineation, we used unpublished digital versions of the geological maps of Qinghai and Yunnan Provinces and Xizang (Tibet) Autonomous Region that were published by the Chinese Ministry of Geology and Mineral Resources in the early 1990s (Bureau of Geology and Mineral Deposits of the Qinghai Province, 1991; Bureau of Geology and Mineral Deposits of the Yunnan Province, 1990; Bureau of Geology and Mineral Deposits of the Xizang Autonomous Region, 1993). The resulting digital geologic map does not always reflect the most recent radiometric age determinations or petrologic studies on the rocks in the tract. At the same time, many of the rocks have not been dated precisely nor studied extensively petrologically. In addition, most of the plutons associated with known deposits and prospects in the tract are less than a square kilometer in outcrop area, and thus are not shown on any of the regional maps nor are they included in the digital map.

The tract was defined on the basis of the Qiangtang terrane, bounded in most places by the Jinsa and Bagong-Nujiang sutures and specifically, by the Chesuo and Tuoba faults (Jiang and others, 2006). The tract is bounded on the northwest by the extent of exposed plutonic rocks; the volcanic rocks further west are mostly ultrapotassic lavas (see Guo and others, 2006); any porphyry deposits that might exist in the western part of the Qiangtang terrane are likely to be concealed at depths greater than a kilometer.

After initial delineation, the limited available geophysical and geochemical information were examined to be sure we included any other evidence of unmapped permissive rocks or hydrothermal systems at shallow depths. A smoothing routine was applied to the resulting polygons, and the tract was trimmed by any terrane-bounding faults. We also excluded areas where Tertiary basins were judged to be deeper than 1 km by buffering inward 1 km from the margins of outcrops of post-mineral sedimentary rock and sediment. The tract is shown in Figure A1.

Known Deposits

Information was found for six known porphyry copper deposits in the tract (table A2). There are no accurate published coordinates nor detailed maps of most of the deposits, so all locations (other than Yulong, which is plainly visible on satellite imagery) are approximate. They were derived by interpolation of page-size maps and inference from satellite imagery.

The known deposits in the tract define a 150 km-long belt in the southern part of the tract (fig. A1). All plutons associated with the deposits have small outcrop areas (< 1 km²), and take the form of small pipe-like bodies. Most are composed of monzogranite, syenogranite, and alkali-feldspar granite, and they characteristically contain biotite as a prominent phenocryst (Hou and others, 2003; Gu and others, 2003). A general description of the Yulong belt is provided by Tang and Luo (1995).

Yulong, the largest deposit, and the most northerly, was first discovered in 1966 (Chen and others, 2009). Singer and others (2008) provide a resource number of 850,000,000 metric tons (t) at 0.84 percent copper, 0.022 percent molybdenite, and 0.35 grams per metric ton (g/t) gold (7,140,000 t of contained copper), although Wang and others (2010), who did a 3-D modeling study of the deposit, report a slightly smaller initial reserve of 6,570,000 tons of copper. A 2006 press release claimed a prospective resource of around 10,000,000 t of copper (Anonymous, 2006) and Wang and others (2010) confirm that number, calling it a "long-term" reserve. The deposit crops out at the surface, and a substantial part of the orebody has been lost to erosion.

Two important types of ore are present—a pipe-like porphyry copper orebody within the stock that is made up of quartz-chalcopyrite-molybdenite veinlets and a supergene-enriched chalcocite-malachite blanket that surrounds the stock near the surface (Hou and others, 2007a). This enrichment blanket, with grades as high as 10 percent copper, is primarily responsible for the overall high grade of the Yulong deposit. Wang and others (2010) show that oxidized ore constitutes nearly 20 percent of the total copper at Yulong. There are also small skarn ore bodies adjacent to the porphyry. Mine construction began in 2006 and production was expected to start in 2010 (Anonymous, 2006), an expectation that appears to have been realized. Figure A2, based on August 2010 imagery, shows the initial mining of dark red oxidized ore on the margin of the deposit.

The Yulong deposit is emplaced into Triassic clastic and carbonate rocks (Ge and others, 1990; Chen and others, 2009). The pluton associated with the deposit has an exposed surface area of less than 1 km² and contains between 63 and 67 percent silica. Sulfur isotopic composition is enriched, indicating a mantle source, and the oxygen and hydrogen isotopic composition indicates derivation from magmatic water (Chen and others, 2009).

Table A2.   Porphyry copper deposits in tract 142pCu8710, Yulong—China.

[Ma, million years; Mt, million metric tons; t, metric ton; g/t, gram per metric ton; Cu-Mo subtype, deposits that have Au/Mo ratios <3 or average Mo grades >0.03 percent; Cu-Au subtype, deposits that have Au/Mo ratios > 30 or average Au grades >0.2 g/t; n.d., no data, NA, not applicable; %, percent. Contained Cu in metric tons is computed as tonnage (Mt × 1,000,000) × Cu grade (percent)]

Name	Latitude	Longitude	Subtype	Age (Ma)	Tonnage (Mt)	Cu (%)	Mo (%)	Au (g/t)	Ag (g/t)	Contained Cu (t)	Reference
Yulong	31.40	97.73	Cu-Au	40.7	850	0.84	0.022	0.35	n.d.	7,140,000	Singer and others (2008), Hou and others (2006, 2007)
Zhanaga	31.20	97.80	NA	38.5	99.5	0.32	0.03	0.03	n.d.	318,000	Hou and others (2003), Liang and others (2006), Yan and others (2007)
Mangzhong	31.17	97.89	NA	37.5	135	0.43	0.03	0.02	n.d.	581,000	Hou and others (2003), Liang and others (2006), Yan and others (2007)
Duoxiasongduo	31.04	97.97	NA	37.4	248	0.38	0.04	0.06	n.d.	942,000	Hou and others (2003), Liang and others (2006), Yan and others (2007)
Malasongduo	30.99	98.02	NA	36.0	338	0.45	0.014	0.06	n.d.	1,520,000	Singer and others (2008), Hou and others, (2006, 2007)
Gegongnong	30.44	98.56	Cu-Au	38.0	101	0.5	n.d.	0.37	2.65	505,000	Singer and others (2008), Anonymous (2003)

Figure A2.   Google Earth™ view of the Yulong porphyry copper deposit, Xizang (Tibet), China. Note the initial open pit in dark red oxidized ore.

Hydrothermal alteration is typical for porphyry copper deposits, with a potassic core, surrounded by a phyllic envelope. High-temperature assemblages include magnetite, indicating an oxidizing environment (Liang and others, 2009a). In addition, advanced argillic alteration has overprinted much of the deposit, and alunite-bearing assemblages are present (Hou and others, 2007a). The pluton at Yulong has a zircon U-Pb age of about 41 Ma as reported by Hou and others (2006, 2007a) and between 44 and 43 Ma by Wang and others (2009). The Re-Os age of molybdenite is 40.7 Ma as reported by Hou and others (2006).

Zhanaga, about 18 km southeast of Yulong, is a much smaller and lower grade deposit that contains about 99,500,000 t of ore, with a copper grade of 0.32 percent, molybdenum of 0.03 percent, and gold of 0.03 g/t (Singer and others, 2008; Yan and others, 2007). Rocks associated with this deposit display potassic, phyllic, argillic, and propylitic hydrothermal alteration zones, but few other details are available (Hou and others, 2003; Gu and others, 2003). Zircons from the host pluton have been dated by Liang and others (2005) at about 38.5 Ma.

Mangzhong is about 25 km southeast of Yulong. It is also small, and contains about 135,000,000 t of ore, with a copper grade of 0.43 percent, molybdenum of 0.03 percent, and gold of 0.02 g/t (Singer and others, 2008; Yan and others, 2007). Rocks at Mangzhong also display potassic, phyllic, argillic, and propylitic hydrothermal alteration zones. It is characterized by associated sphalerite and galena, but few other details are available (Hou and others, 2003; Gu and others, 2003). Zircons from the host pluton have been dated by Liang and others (2005) at about 37.5 Ma.

Duoxiasongduo, about 40 km southeast of Yulong, is somewhat larger; it contains about 248,000,000 t of ore, with a copper grade of 0.38 percent, molybdenum of 0.04 percent, and gold of 0.06 g/t (Singer and others, 2008; Yan and others, 2007). Rocks here display potassic, phyllic, argillic, and propylitic hydrothermal alteration zones, but few other details are available (Hou and others, 2003; Gu and others, 2003). Zircons from the host pluton have been dated by Liang and others (2005) at about 37.4 Ma.

Malasongduo is about 50 km southeast of Yulong, and contains a resource of about 338,000,000 tons of ore, with a copper grade of 0.45 percent, molybdenum of 0.014 percent, and gold of 0.06 g/t (Singer and others, 2008; Yan and others, 2007). A general study on the deposit by Liang and others (2009b) asserts that it is the second largest deposit in the Yulong belt. The associated igneous rocks include both quartz monzonite and more felsic K-feldspar porphyry, all dated at about 37 Ma by U-Pb methods on zircon, whereas the Re-Os age of molybdenite from the deposit is about 36 Ma (Liang and others, 2005). There is a zone of Ag-Pb-Zn enrichment on the outer margins of the porphyry, but few other details are available (Hou and others, 2003; Gu and others, 2003).

Gegongnong is further south, about 135 km southeast of Yulong. Singer and others (2008) list a resource of 101,000,000 t with a copper grade of 0.5 percent, gold of 0.37 g/t, and silver of 2.65 g/t. Much of the ore is in breccia pipes within the quartz monzonite porphyry that hosts the ore and in skarns along the pluton margin (Ding and others, 2005). Gegongnong

has an associated buried placer gold deposit, Maqu, which lies to the north of Gegongnong (Wang and others, 2000). Exploration here is apparently ongoing (Anonymous, 2003). A Rb-Sr age of about 40 Ma and a K-Ar age of about 38 Ma have been reported by Hou and others (2003).

Prospects, Mineral Occurrences, and Related Deposit Types

We have some information on seven porphyry copper prospects within the tract (table A3). There are no accurate published coordinates nor detailed maps of most of these prospects, so all locations were derived by interpolation of page-size maps and inference from satellite imagery and are approximate.

Narigongma, the northernmost prospect in the tract, is located about 360 km northwest of the Yulong deposit, in Qinghai province. Although no grade and tonnage data are available, it is a molybdenum-rich deposit, and is zoned from a molybdenum-rich core to a copper-rich outer zone (Hao and others, 2010a). A cross-section (fig. 7 in Guo and others (2010)) indicates that a substantial part of the mineralized body has been removed by erosion. Guo and others (2010) also provide a table of analyses that demonstrates that many of the intrusive rocks at Narigongma are more silicic than most of the other Yulong belt porphyries, although they are nevertheless best classified as high-K calc-alkaline.

The biotite granite stock at the deposit has an age of 43.3 Ma (Yang and others, 2008), whereas the mineralization age obtained by Re-Os methods is 40.8 Ma (Wang and others, 2008). There is a strong copper anomaly at Narigongma on the copper geochemical map of China (China Geological Survey, 2010b).

Ridanguo is about 120 km northwest of the Yulong deposit. Details about the geology are few, but both Hou and others (2003) and Gu and others (2003) list Ridanguo as an ore-bearing porphyry. Hou and others (2003) determined a K-Ar age on feldspar from the Ridanguo pluton of about 42 Ma.

Xiariduo and Hengxingcuo are further south, about 45 and 15 km, respectively, northwest of the Yulong deposit. No specific descriptions of the deposits are available, but they are both listed as ore-bearing porphyries by Hou and others (2003) and Gu and others (2003). In addition, Jiang and others (2008) provide major- and trace-element analyses of the monzogranite porphyries associated with these prospects, and group them with their ore-bearing porphyries. Hou and others (2003) report K-Ar ages for Xiariduo of about 46 Ma and for Hengxingcuo of about 41 Ma.

Seli, Jucuo, and Mamupu (which includes the Zengxi area mentioned by Gu and others (2003)) are all south of the known deposits in the tract. Seli is about 30 km south, Jicuo is about 50 km south, and Mamupu about 60 km south of Gegongnong, the southernmost porphyry copper deposit in the tract. All these igneous centers are more alkaline and have lower silica contents than those that host the known deposits; they include syenites and are distinctly shoshonitic

Table A3. Significant prospects and occurrences in tract 142pCu8710, Yulong—China.

[Ma, million years; Mt, million metric tons; %, percent; g/t, grams per metric ton]

Name	Latitude	Longitude	Age (Ma)	Comments (grade and tonnage data, if available)	Reference
Narigongma	33.53	94.78	41	discovered after 2000; Mo-rich	Wang and others (2008), Yang and others (2008)
Ridanguo	32.15	96.77	42	"ore-bearing" porphyry	Hou and others (2003), Gu and others (2003), Jiang and others (2006), Singer and others (2008)
Xiariduo	31.68	97.45	46	"ore-bearing" porphyry	Hou and others (2003), Gu and others (2003), Jiang and others (2006), Singer and others (2008)
Hengxingcuo	31.46	97.60	41	"ore-bearing" porphyry	Hou and others (2003), Gu and others (2003), Jiang and others (2006), Singer and others (2008)
Seli	30.14	98.45	36	"ore-bearing" porphyry	Hou and others (2003), Gu and others (2003), Jiang and others (2006), Singer and others (2008)
Mamupu	29.96	98.53	38	Cu 0.12–0.32%; Au 6.4–13.1 g/t; no tonnage; includes Zengxi and Jicuo	Hou and others (2003), Gu and others (2003), Jiang and others (2006), Singer and others (2008)
Lurige	33.42	95.00	Eocene?	newly discovered porphyry Mo-Cu prospect	Hao and others (2010)

(Jiang and others, 2008). Mamupu was discovered using stream-sediment geochemistry (Cheng and others, 2005). Seli is apparently undated, but the Mamupu complex has an age of about 38 Ma (Hou and others, 2003).

The Lurige prospect is described by Hao and others (2010b) as a newly discovered molybdenum (copper) porphyry deposit in Yushu County of Qinghai province, to the southeast of Narigongma. The location reported here is very uncertain, as is its classification, since no grade information is available. Lurige is not included in figure A1. Nevertheless its presence documents hydrothermal mineralization related to high-level intrusions. Hao and others (2010b) provide geochemical and isotopic data on the intrusions at Lurige and conclude that the rocks are calc-alkaline and include both mantle and crustal contributions to their composition. No information about grades of the mineralized rock is available.

Exploration History

Exploration for porphyry copper deposits in this tract is at a relatively early stage, as the porphyry copper model was not well-known in China until the 1960s, when scientific and industrial activity was renewed after a long period of warfare and internal turmoil. Since that time, basic geologic mapping, as well as detailed geochemical and geophysical surveys have been completed, resulting in the discovery of numerous known deposits and prospects. Yulong was the first discovery in this area; it was recognized by outcropping malachite in 1966. There has been extensive exploration for outcropping deposits in the central and southern parts of the tract, but the northwestern part is still remote and poorly known, as evidenced by the recent discovery of the Narigongma prospect. In addition, post-mineral sediment and sedimentary rocks

cover large areas. There is little evidence that non-Chinese exploration companies are operating in this part of China.

Stream-sediment geochemical surveys conducted by the China Geological Survey have been instrumental in discovery of many of the deposits and prospects in this tract. A nationwide geochemical map for copper (China Geological Survey, 2010b) shows prominent anomalies coincident with the Narigongma, Xiariduo, Yulong, Zhanaga, Duoxiasongduo, Malasongduo, Gegongnong, and Mamupu areas. Numerous other anomalies, not associated with known deposits or prospects, are displayed on this map, both in the southeastern and northwestern part of the tract.

Sources of Information

Principal sources of information used by the assessment team for delineation of the tract are listed in table A4. No geophysical data at an appropriate scale were available for the assessment.

Grade and Tonnage Model Selection

There are six known deposits in the tract, and we compared their tonnage and grades statistically to the worldwide deposit models of Singer and others (2008). Some, but not all of the deposits in the tract are gold-rich, but the Yulong deposits have distinctly higher Mo grades than the deposits included in the Cu-Au model. On the other hand, the Yulong deposits have distinctly higher Au grades than the deposits included in the Cu-Mo model. The general porphyry copper grade and tonnage model was judged to be the most appropriate model, and it was used for the estimation of undiscovered resources in the Yulong tract. Results of the *t*-test analysis used are shown in table A5.

Table A4.   Principal sources of information used for tract 142pCu8710, Yulong—China.

[NA, not applicable]

Theme	Name or Title	Scale	Citation
Geology	Regional geology of Qinghai Province	1:1,000,000	Bureau of Geology and Mineral Resources of the Qinghai Province (1991)
	Regional geology of Xizang (Tibet) Autonomous Region	1:500,000	Bureau of Geology and Mineral Resources of the Xizang Autonomous Region (1993)
	Regional geology of Yunnan Province	1:1,000,000	Bureau of Geology and Mineral Resources of the Yunnan Province (1990)
Mineral occurrences	Porphyry copper deposits of the world: database, map, and grade and tonnage models	NA	Singer and others (2008)
	Metal Mining Agency of Japan mineral deposit database	NA	Metal Mining Agency of Japan (1998)
	World Minerals Geoscience database	NA	Natural Resources Canada (2010); Kirkham and Dunne (2000)
	Geological Survey of Japan mineral resources map of East Asia	NA	Kamitani and others (2007)
	The Himalayan Yulong porphyry copper belt—Product of large-scale strike-slip faulting in eastern Tibet	NA	Hou and others (2003)
	Himalayan magmatism and porphyry copper-molybdenum mineralization in the Yulong ore belt, East Tibet	NA	Gu and others (2003)
Stream-sediment geochemistry	Copper geochemical map	1: 12,000,000	China Geological Survey (2010b)
	Bismuth geochemical map	1: 12,000,000	China Geological Survey (2010a)

Table A5.   Statistical test results for tract 142pCu8710, Yulong, China.

[Pooled t-test results assuming equal variances; ANOVA tests used for tracts with a single deposit; $p > 0.01$ indicates that the deposits in the tract are not significantly different from those in the model at the 1-percent level; $p < 0.01$ indicates that the deposits in the tract are significantly different from those in the model at the 1-percent level and therefore, the tract fails the selected test (*) and the model is inappropriate for the assessment. N_{known}, number of known deposits in the tract. Note that silver is reported for only 1 of the 6 known deposits]

Coded_ID	Tract name	N_{known}	Model	p values					Model selected	Basis for selection
				Tons	Cu	Mo	Ag	Au		
142pCu8710	Yulong	6	Cu-Au-Mo	0.87	0.71	0.09	0.74	0.22	Cu-Au-Mo	t-test results
			Cu-Mo	0.31	0.84	0.83	0.54	*0.0027		
			Cu-Au	0.89	0.77	*<0.001	0.88	*<0.001		

Estimate of the Number of Undiscovered Deposits

Rationale for the Estimate

There are six known deposits and at least six porphyry copper prospects in the Yulong tract. However, Hou and others (2003) state that the Yulong belt contains "dozens of minor prospects and mineralized porphyry intrusions." The density of deposits and prospects along the best-explored part of the trend (from Xiariduo to Mamupu) is quite remarkable—ten mineralized systems in 230 km. The area in the northwest part of the tract is probably underexplored, as it is remote and difficult to access due to the climate, the altitude, and a lack of infrastructure. Continued exploration in the Yulong belt is likely to result in additional discoveries.

Based in part on the presence of at least six prospects in a productive area, the team estimated that there was a 90 percent chance of 3 or more undiscovered deposits in the tract; we believe that several of the presently identified prospects will, upon thorough exploration and development, become deposits. At the same time, the relatively small size of the tract limits the total number of undiscovered deposits that might exist there, and the team estimated 18 undiscovered deposits at the 10 percentile confidence level. The estimated mean number of undiscovered deposits is 8.5 (table A6).

Because of the subjective nature of the tract delineation, it could be misleading to place great credence in a calculated deposit density for this tract, but the team's estimate is entirely consistent with worldwide deposit density estimates (Singer, 2008; Singer and others, 2005).

A previous assessment (Yan and others, 2007) covered only the well-mineralized southeast part of the tract (their Tract XI-4a and part of tract XI). They estimated about 3 mean undiscovered deposits, compared with the present team's estimate of 8.5 deposits (table A6). The larger area designated permissive in this study is consistent with the larger estimate. Combined with the 6 known deposits, this means that the tract probably contains 14 or 15 porphyry copper deposits.

Table A6.   Undiscovered deposit estimates, deposit numbers, tract area, and deposit density for tract 142pCu8710, Yulong—China.

[N_{xx}, estimated number of deposits associated with the xxth percentile; N_{und}, expected number of undiscovered deposits; s, standard deviation; $C_v\%$, coefficient of variance; N_{known}, number of known deposits in the tract that are included in the grade and tonnage model; N_{total}, total of expected number of deposits plus known deposits; area, area of permissive tract in square kilometers; density, deposit density reported as the total number of deposits per km². N_{und}, s, and $C_v\%$ are calculated using a regression equation (Singer and Menzie, 2005)]

Consensus undiscovered deposit estimates					Summary statistics					Tract area (km²)	Deposit density (N_{total}/km²)
N_{90}	N_{50}	N_{10}	N_{05}	N_{01}	N_{und}	s	$C_v\%$	N_{known}	N_{total}		
3	6	18	18	18	8.5	5.7	67	6	14	112,470	0.00013

Table A7.   Results of Monte Carlo simulations of undiscovered resources for tract 142pCu8710, Yulong—China.

[Cu, copper; Mo, molybdenum; Au, gold; and Ag, silver; in metric tons; Rock, in million metric tons]

Material	Probability of at least the indicated amount						Probability of	
	0.95	0.9	0.5	0.1	0.05	Mean	Mean or greater	None
Cu (t)	830,000	2,700,000	20,000,000	76,000,000	110,000,000	32,000,000	0.34	0.03
Mo (t)	0	14,000	380,000	2,300,000	3,600,000	910,000	0.28	0.07
Au (t)	0	30	470	2,000	2,700	820	0.33	0.06
Ag (t)	0	0	4,200	27,000	42,000	11,000	0.27	0.11
Rock (Mt)	210	610	4,200	16,000	22,000	6,600	0.35	0.03

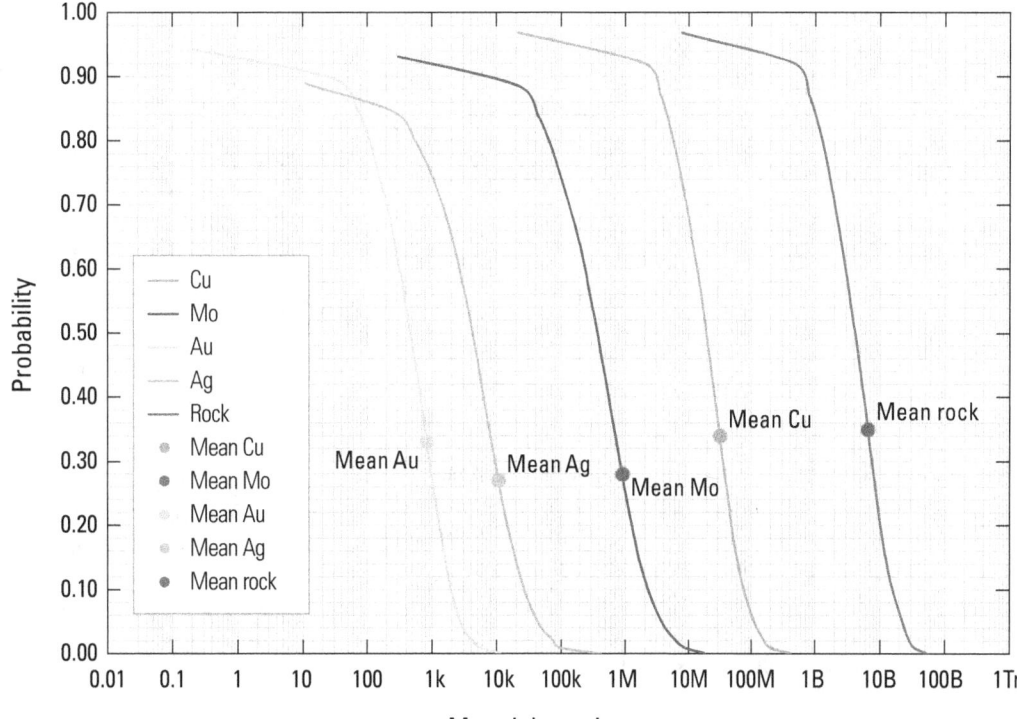

Figure A3.   Cumulative frequency plot showing the results of Monte Carlo computer simulation of undiscovered resources for tract 142pCu8710, Yulong—China. k, thousand; M, million; B, billion; Tr, trillion.

Probabilistic Assessment Simulation Results

Undiscovered resources for the tract were estimated by combining the team's estimate for numbers of undiscovered porphyry copper deposits with the general porphyry copper model of Singer and others (2008) using the EMINERS program (Root and others, 1992; Bawiec and Spanski, 2012; Duval, 2012). Selected simulation results are reported in table A7. Results of the Monte Carlo simulation are presented as a cumulative frequency plot (fig. A3), which shows the estimated resource amounts associated with cumulative probabilities of occurrence, as well as the mean, for each commodity and for total mineralized rock.

References Cited

Anonymous, 2003, China NetTV Holdings Inc.—Acquisition of Honglu, a company with mining properties in China: World Tibet Network News, July 9, 2003, accessed December 5, 2010, at www.tibet.ca/en/newsroom/wtn/archive/old?y=2003&m=7&p=9_3.

Anonymous, 2006, New copper mine to open as prices skyrocket: Asia Times, April 4, 2006, accessed December 5, 2010, at http://www.atimes.com/atimes/China_Business/HD07Cb01.html.

Bawiec, W.J., and Spanski, G.T., 2012, Quick-start guide for version 3.0 of EMINERS—Economic Mineral Resource Simulator: U.S. Geological Survey Open-File Report 2009–1057, 26 p., accessed June 30, 2012, at http://pubs.usgs.gov/of/2009/1057. (This report supplements USGS OFR 2004–1344.)

Bureau of Geology and Mineral Resources of the Qinghai Province, 1991, Regional Geology of Qinghai Province: Geological Memoirs, series 1, no. 24, Geological Publishing House, Beijing, 662 p. [Includes geological maps at 1:1,000,000 scale, magmatic rock maps at 1:2,000,000 scale, and geological structure maps at 1:2,000,000 scale.]

Bureau of Geology and Mineral Resources of the Xizang Autonomous Region, 1993, Regional Geology of Xizang (Tibet) Autonomous Region—Geological Memoirs, series 1, no. 31: Geological Publishing House, Beijing, 707 p. [Includes geological maps at 1:500,000 scale, magmatic rock maps at 1:2,000,000 scale, and tectonic maps at 1:2,000,000 scale.]

Bureau of Geology and Mineral Resources of the Yunnan Province, 1990, Regional Geology of Yunnan Province—Geological Memoirs, series 1, no. 21: Geological Publishing House, Beijing, 728 p. [Includes geological maps at 1:1,000,000 scale, magmatic maps at 1:1,000,000 scale, metamorphic maps at 1:2,000,000 scale, and geological structure maps at 1:1,000,000 scale.]

Chen, Jianping, Tang, Juxing, Cong, Yuan, Dong, Qingji, and Hao, Jinhua, 2009, Geological characteristics and metallogenic model in the Yulong porphyry copper deposit, East Tibet: Acta Geologica Sinica, v. 83, p. 1887–1900.

Cheng, Jianxun, Ye, Songqing, Ding, Feng, and Tang, Juxing, 2005, Geochemical anomaly evaluation of porphyry-type Cu-Au-Ag polymetallic mineralization zone of Mamupu, eastern Tibet: Global Geology, v. 24, p. 334–337.

China Geological Survey, 2010a, Bismuth geochemical map: accessed August 13, 2011, at http://www.ngac.cn/Gallery_New/Default.aspx?tab=last&type=image&node=9&id=966.

China Geological Survey, 2010b, Copper geochemical map: accessed August 13, 2011, at http://www.ngac.cn/Gallery_New/Default.aspx?tab=last&type=image&node=13&id=966.

Cox, D.P., 1986, Descriptive model of porphyry Cu, in Cox, D.P., and Singer, D.A., eds., 1986, Mineral deposit models: U.S. Geological Survey Bulletin 1693, p. 76. (Also available at http://pubs.usgs.gov/bul/b1693/.)

Ding, Feng, Tang, Juxing, Huang, Wei, Chen, Shenghua, and Zhang, Jinshu, 2005, Geological characteristics and metallogenesis of the Gegongnong polymetallic copper-gold deposit in the eastern Tibet: Contributions to Geology and Mineral Resources Research, v. 20, p. 15–20. [In Chinese, with English abstract.]

Duval, J.S., 2012, Version 3.0 of EMINERS—Economic Mineral Resource Simulator: U.S. Geological Survey Open-File Report 2004–1344, available at http://pubs.usgs.gov/of/2004/1344.

Ge, Chaohua, Sun, Haitian, and Zhou, Taihe, 1990, Copper deposits of China, in Mineral deposits of China, v. 1: Geological Publishing House, Beijing, p. 1–106. [In Chinese.]

Gu, X.X., Tang, J.X., Wang, C.S., Chen, J.P., and He, B.B., 2003, Himalayan magmatism and porphyry copper-molybdenum mineralization in the Yulong ore belt, East Tibet: Mineralogy and Petrology, v. 78, p. 1–20.

Guo, Guien, Ma, Yanqing, Wang, Tao, Zhang, Yongtao, Ye, Jilong, and Liu, Baoshan, 2010, The formation mechanism and mineralization pattern of ore-bearing granite porphyry in Narigongma: Northwestern Geology, v. 43, p. 28–35. [In Chinese, with English abstract.]

Guo, Zhengfu, Wilson, Marjorie, Liu, Jiaqi, and Mao, Qian, 2006, Post-collisional, potassic and ultrapotassic magmatism of the northern Tibetan Plateau—Constraints on characteristics of the mantle source, geodynamic setting and uplift mechanisms: Journal of Petrology, v. 47, p. 1177–1220.

Hao, Jinhua, Chen, Jianping, Dong, Qingji, Wang, Tao, and Luo, Zhizhong, 2010a, Geochemistry of the ore-bearing porphyry of Lurige Mo(Cu) deposit, Qinghai—Implications for tectonic setting and lithogenesis: Bulletin of Mineralogy, Petrology, and Geochemistry, v. 29, p. 328–354. [In Chinese, with English abstract.]

Hao, Jinhua, Chen, Jianping, Tian, Yongge, Li, Yulong, and Yin, Jingwu, 2010b, Mineralogical features of porphyries in the Narigongma Mo(-Cu) deposit, southern Qinghai and their implications for petrogenesis and mineralization: Geology and Exploration, v. 46, p. 367–376. [In Chinese, with English abstract.]

Hou, Zengqian, Ma, Hongwen, Zaw, Khin, Zhang, Yuquan, Wang, Mingjie, Wang, Zeng, Pan, Guitang, and Tang, Renli, 2003, The Himalayan Yulong porphyry copper belt—Product of large-scale strike-slip faulting in eastern Tibet: Economic Geology, v. 98, p. 125–145.

Hou, Zengqian, Xie, Yuling, Xu, Wenyi, Li, Yinqing, Zhu, Xlangkun, Zaw, Khin, Beaudoin, G., Rui, Zongyao, Huang, Wei, and Luobu, Ciren, 2007a, Yulong deposit, eastern Tibet—A high-sulfidation Cu-Au porphyry copper deposit in the eastern Indo-Asian collision zone: International Geology Review, v. 49, p. 235–258.

Hou, Zengqian, Zaw, Khin, Pan, Guitang, Mo, Xuanxue, Xu, Qiang, Hu, Yunzhong, and Li, Xingzhen, 2007b, Sanjiang Tethyan metallogenesis in S.W. China—Tectonic setting, metallogenic epochs and deposit types: Ore Geology Reviews v. 31, p. 48–87.

Hou, Zengqian, Zeng, Pusheng, Gao, Yongfeng, Du, Andao, and Fu, Deming, 2006, Himalayan Cu–Mo–Au mineralization in the eastern Indo–Asian collision zone—Constraints from Re–Os dating of molybdenite: Mineralium Deposita, v. 41, p. 33–45.

Hou, Zengqian, Zhang, Hongrui, Pan, Xiaofei, and Yang, Zhiming, 2011, Porphyry Cu (-Mo-Au) deposits related to melting of thickened mafic lower crust—Examples from the eastern Tethyan metallogenic domain: Ore Geology Reviews, v. 39, p. 21–45.

Jiang, Yaohui, Jiang, Shaoyong, Dai, Baozhang, and Ling, Hongfei, 2008, Origin of ore-bearing porphyries in the Yulong porphyry copper deposit, East Tibet: Geological Publishing House, Beijing, 122 p. [In Chinese and English.]

Jiang, Yaohui, Jiang, Shaoyong, Ling, Hongfei, and Dai, Baozhang, 2006, Low-degree melting of a metasomatized lithospheric mantle for the origin of Cenozoic Yulong monzogranite-porphyry, east Tibet—Geochemical and Sr-Nd-Pb-Hf isotopic constraints: Earth and Planetary Science Letters, v. 241, p. 617–633.

John, D.A., Ayuso, R.A., Barton, M.D., Blakeley, R.J., Bodnar, R.J., Dilles, J.H., Gray, F., Graybeal, F.T., Mars, J.C., McPhee, D.K., Seal, R.R., Taylor, R.D., and Vikre, P.G., 2010, Porphyry copper deposit model, chap. B of Mineral deposit models for resource assessment: U.S. Geological Survey Scientific Investigations Report 2010-5070-B, 169 p., accessed September 8, 2010, at http://pubs.usgs.gov/sir/2010/5070/b/.

Kamitani, M., Okumura, K., Teraoka, Y., Miyano, S., and Watanabe, Y., 2007, Mineral Resources Map of East Asia: Geological Survey of Japan, data sheet and explanatory notes, accessed February 8, 2010, at http://www.gsj.jp/Map/EN/docs/overseas_doc/mrm-e_asia.htm.

Kirkham, R.V., and Dunne, K.P.E., 2000, World distribution of porphyry, porphyry-associated skarn, and bulk-tonnage epithermal deposits and occurrences: Geological Survey of Canada Open File 3792a, 26 p.

Liang, Huaying, Mo, Jihai, Sun, Weidong, Zhang, Yuquan, Zeng, Ti, Hu, Guangqian, and Allen, C.M., 2009b, Study on geochemical composition and isotope ages of the Malasongduo porphyry associated with Cu-Mo mineralization: Acta Petrologica Sinica, v. 25, p. 385–392. [In Chinese, with English abstract.]

Liang, Huaying, Sun, Weidong, Su, Wenchao, and Zartman, Robert E., 2009a, Porphyry copper-gold mineralization at Yulong, China, promoted by decreasing redox potential during magnetite alteration: Economic Geology, v. 104, p. 587–596.

Liang, Huaying, Zhang, Yuqiang, Xie, Yingwen, Lin, Wu, Campbell, I.H., and Yu, Hengxiang, 2005, Geochronological and geochemical study on the Yulong porphyry copper ore belt in eastern Tibet, China: Mineral Deposit Research—Meeting the Global Challenge, Proceedings of the Eighth Biennial SGA, Beijing, 2005, v. 1, p. 1235–1237.

Metal Mining Agency of Japan (MMAJ), 1998, Mineral resources map of Asia: Metal Mining Agency of Japan, 1 sheet and 43 p.

Natural Resources Canada, 2010, World minerals geoscience database: accessed February 8, 2010, at http://gsc nrcan.gc.ca/wmgdb/index_e.php.

Root, D.H., Menzie, W.D., and Scott, W.A., 1992, Computer Monte Carlo simulation in quantitative resource estimation: Natural Resources Research, v. 1, no. 2, p. 125–138.

Singer, D.A., 2008, Mineral deposit densities for estimating mineral resources: Mathematical Geosciences, v. 40, p. 33–46.

Singer, D.A., Berger, V.I., and Moring, B.C., 2008, Porphyry copper deposits of the world: U.S. Geological Survey Open-File Report 2008–1155, 45 p., accessed August 10, 2009, at http://pubs.usgs.gov/of/2008/1155/.

Singer, D.A., Berger, V.I., Menzie, W.D., and Berger, B.R., 2005, Porphyry copper density: Economic Geology, v. 100, no. 3, p. 491–514.

Singer, D.A. and Menzie, W.D., 2005, Statistical guides to estimating the number of undiscovered mineral deposits—An example with porphyry copper deposits, *in* Cheng, Qiuming, and Bonham-Carter, Graeme, eds., Proceedings of IAMG—The annual conference of the International Association for Mathematical Geology: Toronto, Canada, Geomatics Research Laboratory, York University, p. 1028–1033.

Tang, Renli, and Luo, Huaisong, 1995, The geology of Yulong porphyry copper (molybdenum) ore belt, Xizang (Tibet): Beijing, Geological Publishing House, 320 p. [In Chinese.]

U.S. Department of State, 2009, Small-scale digital international land boundaries (SSIB)—Lines, edition 10, and polygons, beta edition 1, *in* Boundaries and sovereignty encyclopedia (B.A.S.E.): U.S. Department of State, Office of the Geographer and Global Issues.

Wang, Chenghui, Tang, Juxing, Chen, Jianping, Hao, Jinhua, Gao, Yiming, Liuy, Yaowen, Fan, Tao, Zhang, Qizhi, Ying, Lijuan, and Chen, Zhijiao, 2009, Chronological research of Yulong copper-molybdenum porphyry deposit: Acta Geologica Sinica, v. 83, p. 1445–1455. [In Chinese, with English abstract.]

Wang, Limei, Chen, Jianping, and Tang, Juxing, 2010, 3D positioning and quantitative prediction of Yulong porphyry copper deposit, Tibet, China, based on digital mineral deposit model: Geological Bulletin of China, v. 29, p. 565–570. [In Chinese, with English abstract.]

Wang, Qian, Huang, Wei, Tang, Juxing, Xin, Zhonglei, and Lin, Fang, 2000, Geologic characteristics of the Maqu placer gold deposit, Gonjo, eastern Tibet: Journal of Chengdu University of Technology, v. 27, p. 328–330. [In Chinese, with English abstract.]

Wang, Zhao Lin, Yang, Zhi Ming, Yang, Zhu Sen, Tian, Shi Hon, Liu, Ying Chao, Ma, Yan Qing, Wang, Gui Ren, and Qu, Wen Jun, 2008, Narigongma porphyry molybdenite copper deposit, northern extension of Yulong copper belt—Evidence from the age of Re-Os isotope: Acta Petrologica Sinica, 2008-03. [In Chinese, with English abstract.]

Yan, Guangsheng, Qiu, Ruizhao, Lian, Changyun, Nokleberg, Warren J., Cao, Li, Chen Xiufa, Mao, Jingwen, Xiao, Keyan, Li, Jinyi, Xiao, Qinghui, Zhou, Su, Wang, Mingyan, Liu, Dawen, Yuan, Chunhua, Han, Jiuxi, Wang, Liangliang, Chen, Zhen, Chen, Yuming, Xie, Guiqing, and Ding, Jianhua, 2007, Quantitative assessment of the resource potential of porphyry copper systems in China: Earth Science Frontiers, v. 14, p. 27–41.

Yang, Zhiming, Hou, Zenqian, Yang, Zhushen, Wang, Shuxian, Wang, Guiren, Tian, Shihong, Wen, Deyin, Wng, Zhaolin, and Liu, Yingchao, 2008, Genesis of porphyries and tectonic controls on the Narigongma porphyry Mo(-Cu) deposit, southern Qinghai: Acta Petrologica Sinica, v. 24, p. 489–502. [In Chinese, with English abstract.]

Appendix B. Porphyry Copper Assessment for Tract 142pCu8711, Dali—China and Vietnam

By Steve Ludington[1], Jane M. Hammarstrom[2], Gilpin R. Robinson, Jr.[2], and Robert J. Miller[1], based on contributions of Yan Guangsheng[3], Peng Qiuming[3], Lian Changyun[3], Mao Jingwen[4], Li Jinyi[3], Xiao Keyan[3], Qiu Ruizhao[3], Shao Jianbao[3], Shai Gangyi[3], and Du Yuliang[3]

Deposit Type Assessed: Porphyry Copper

Deposit type: Porphyry copper
Descriptive model: Porphyry copper (Cox, 1986; John and others, 2010)
Grade and tonnage model: Gold-rich porphyry copper (Singer and others, 2008)
Table B1 summarizes selected assessment results.

Table B1.   Summary of selected resource assessment results for tract 142pCu8711, Dali—China.

[km, kilometers; km^2, square kilometers; t, metric tons]

Date of assessment	Assessment depth (km)	Tract area (km^2)	Known copper resource (t)	Mean estimate of undiscovered copper resources (t)	Median estimate of undiscovered copper resources (t)
2010	1	96,670	490,000	26,000,000	15,000,000

Location

The Dali tract extends for nearly 1,000 kilometers (km), from northern to southern Yunnan Province in China and into Vietnam, along the Sanjiang-Red River transform fault zone, and includes an eastward extension about 300 km into southwestern Sichuan Province on the South China craton (fig. B1). The tract is exceedingly mountainous, with elevations ranging from nearly 6,000 meters (m) to less than 1,000 m.

Geologic Feature Assessed

An assemblage of Eocene and Oligocene igneous rocks that formed in a transtensional post-subduction environment in southwest China during the collision between India and Asia.

---

[1]U.S. Geological Survey, Menlo Park, California, United States.
[2]U.S. Geological Survey, Reston, Virginia, United States.
[3]China Geological Survey, Beijing, China.
[4]Chinese Academy of Geological Sciences, Beijing, China.

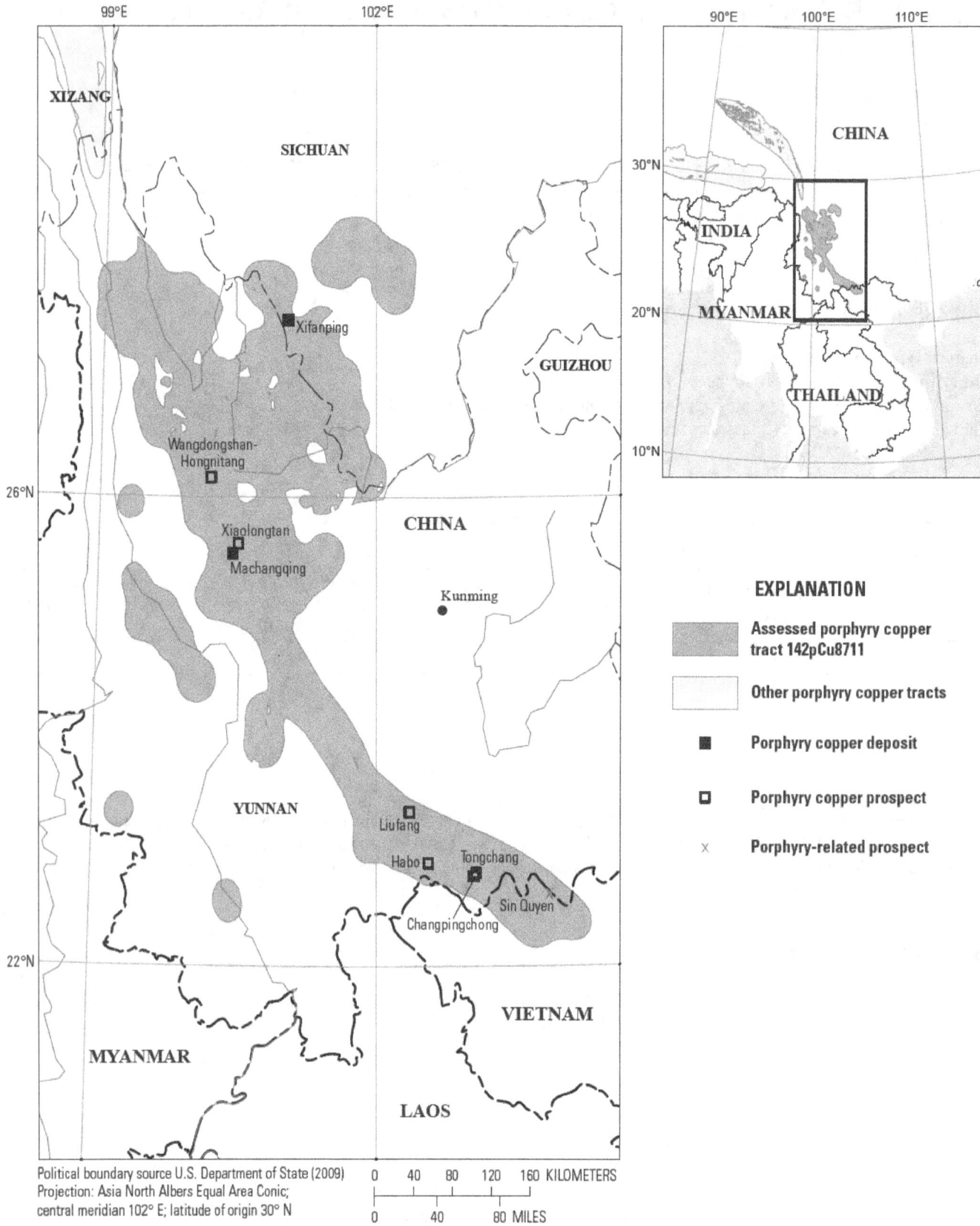

Figure B1.   Map showing tract location, known porphyry copper deposits, and significant porphyry copper prospects for tract 142pCu8711, Dali—China and Vietnam.

Delineation of the Permissive Tract

Geologic Criteria

Igneous rocks that define the Dali tract formed during continental-scale strike-slip faulting during the late-collision stage. These rocks range in age from about 40 million years (Ma) to about 26 Ma (see Deng and others, 1998), and are therefore slightly younger than the rocks in the Yulong porphyry belt to the north. They were emplaced along the Sanjiang-Red River fault zone, the southern extension of the Jinsa suture which forms the boundary between Indochina and the South China craton and constitutes the suture between them (Wang and others, 2001b; Guo and others, 2005). The rocks also extend several hundred kilometers eastward onto the South China craton. In addition, REE-bearing carbonatite complexes with ages between about 40 and 10 Ma crop out along the eastern margin of the tract (Hou and others, 2009).

The Sanjiang-Red River structure is a strike-slip fault that has accommodated much of the strain associated with the Indo-Asian collision since the Paleocene; there are numerous strands of this fault. All but one (Xifanping) of the two porphyry copper deposits and eight prospects in the tract are within about 50 km of this structure.

Most of the igneous rocks form porphyritic intrusions, though a few volcanic remnants crop out. The majority of the plutons are syenite, but include some granite and monzonite, as well as numerous small bodies of mafic alkaline rock (Deng and others, 1998; Wu and others, 2005; Guo and others, 2005). These rocks, emplaced between about 40 and 26 Ma, appear to have formed by melting metasomatized mantle at depths near 100 km (Guo and others, 2005). This melting was triggered by the large trans-crustal strike-slip faults that traverse and help define the tract (Hou and others, 2005, 2010).

As a basis for tract delineation, we used unpublished digital versions of the geological maps of Yunnan and Sichuan Province published by the Chinese Ministry of Geology and Mineral Resources in the early 1990s (Bureau of Geology and Mineral Deposits of the Yunnan Province, 1990; Bureau of Geology and Mineral Deposits of the Sichuan Province, 1991). The resulting digital geologic map does not always reflect the most recent radiometric age determinations or petrologic studies on the rocks in the tract, whose ages are not always accurately known. At the same time, many of the rocks have not been dated precisely nor been studied extensively petrologically. In addition, many of the plutons associated with known deposits and prospects in the tract are less than a square kilometer in outcrop area, and are not included in the digital map.

To define the area included in the permissive tract, we first classified igneous map units as permissive or not, based on the geologic criteria described above, i.e. calc-alkaline and alkaline volcanic and plutonic rocks of Tertiary age. The plutons that help define the tract are primarily syenite, but include lesser amounts of granite, monzonite, and diorite. Volcanic rocks in the tract are far less abundant than plutons; they are predominantly trachyte, but include minor dacite and rhyolite. In addition to these polygons from the digital geologic map,

we digitized additional polygons to represent those bodies shown in figure 1 of Guo and others (2005) but not present on the digital map. These are all mafic alkaline rocks. We also compared the tract to the generalized map in figure 1 of Yang (2010) and to map 17 of Wagner (2003) to ensure the inclusion of all the alkaline plutons on those maps.

A 20-km buffer was applied to plutonic rock polygons and a 2-km buffer to volcanic rock polygons. Buffering expanded the area of the tract to include the prospects in the tract and account for uncertainties in the cartographic position of mapped boundaries, as well as possible unexposed or unmapped permissive rocks. A larger 20-km buffer was chosen for this tract because so many of the igneous bodies are small and often not portrayed on regional maps.

After initial delineation, the limited available geophysical and geochemical information was examined to be sure that any other evidence of unmapped permissive rocks or hydrothermal systems at shallow depths was included. A corridor along the Ailoshan suture was also included, which controlled the emplacement of the igneous rocks. A smoothing routine was applied to the resulting polygons, and the tract was trimmed to terrane-bounding faults. Areas where Tertiary basins were judged to be deeper than 1 km were excluded by buffering inward 1 km from the margins of outcrops of post-mineral sedimentary rock and sediment. The tract is shown in figure B1.

Chen and others (2007) conducted a mineral resource assessment in the region based on weights of evidence (Bonham-Carter and others, 1989). Because their method relied heavily on geochemical information, it was problematic to separate copper anomalies due to basalt-related copper deposits in the area from those that might be due to porphyry-style mineralization. Nevertheless, they identified a number of prospective areas for polymetallic deposits that correspond closely to the southern arm of the geology-based tract we delineated. The tract corresponds generally to the Jinshajiang-Ailoshan Cu-Au metallogenic belt, as defined by Wang and others (2009).

Known Deposits

The tract contains two known porphyry copper deposits (table B2). These deposits are named Xifanping and Machangqing.

Xifanping (also known as Mofancun), the northernmost deposit in the tract, is in western Sichuan Province. It is briefly described by Hou and others (2006) as being related to a multistage quartz monzonite pluton, with an associated breccia pipe (Li and others, 2006). Xiao and others (1999) studied the intrusions in more detail and identified at least 130 individual bodies, many with outcrop areas less than 0.1 km^2. Compositions of the intrusions range from quartz syenite to quartz monzonite; the rocks are commonly altered to assemblages that include sericite and chlorite. Ore is within and on the periphery of the stocks; molybdenum is concentrated in early-formed veins in the K-silicate alteration zone and gold is concentrated in later peripheral veins. The deposit is small, but the gold grade is 0.31 grams per metric ton (g/t) (Singer and others, 2008). Xifanping also includes a supergene chalcocite-bearing enrichment blanket that is as much as 100 meters (m) thick and contains grades up

Table B2.   Porphyry copper deposits in tract 142pCu8711, Dali—China and Vietnam.

[Ma, million years; Mt, million metric tons; t, metric ton; g/t, gram per metric ton; Cu-Mo subtype, deposits that have Au/Mo ratios <3 or average Mo grades >0.03 percent; Cu-Au subtype, deposits that have Au/Mo ratios > 30 or average Au grades >0.2 g/t; n.d., no data, NA, not applicable. Contained Cu in metric tons is computed as tonnage (Mt × 1,000,000) × Cu grade (percent)]

Name	Latitude	Longitude	Subtype	Age (Ma)	Tonnage (Mt)	Cu (%)	Mo (%)	Au (g/t)	Ag (g/t)	Contained Cu (t)	Reference
Xifanping	27.491	101.017	Cu-Au	32	64.3	0.28	n.d.	0.31	n.d.	180,000	Singer and others (2008), Hou and others (2006)
Machangqing	25.521	100.438	unk	35	62	0.5	0.078	0.35	n.d.	310,000	Singer and others (2008), Peng and others (1998), Hou and others (2006), Wang and others (2005)

to 0.8 percent copper (Wang and others, 2001a). Re-Os dating indicates a mineralization age of about 32 Ma (Hou and others, 2006; Zeng and others, 2006).

Yanyuan is mentioned in a single paper (Chen and others, 1996), and Kirkham and Dunne (2000) suggest a location just 10 km south of Xifanping. However their location for Xifanping is 35 km east of its actual location. Because there is no post-1996 mention of this deposit, and because Xifanping is in Yanyuan county, we think it likely that Yanyuan is another name for Xifanping and is thus not shown on figure B1.

Machangqing is located about 200 km south of Xifanping, in northern Yunnan, and is probably the most thoroughly studied deposit in the tract. The deposit is described by Peng and others (1998) as being related to an I-type granite porphyry stock, intruded by monzonite porphyry and lamprophyre dikes. Three types of ore are present in the district, porphyry Cu-Mo within the stock, skarn Cu-Mo-Au on the margins of the stock, and epithermal gold-polymetallic more distal in the Ordovician calcareous sedimentary wall rocks (Guo and others, 2009, 2010; Wang and others, 2010). A cross-section (fig. 5 of Peng and others, 1998) implies that a large part of the deposit may have been removed by erosion, perhaps helping to explain its small size. The reported distribution of hydrothermal alteration assemblages is typical for porphyry copper deposits, and hydrothermal magnetite is abundant. The deposit is rich in both gold (0.35 g/t) and molybdenum (0.078 percent) (Singer and others, 2008).

In two separate studies (Hou and others, 2006; Wang and others, 2005), Machangqing was dated by the Re-Os method to be about 35–34 Ma, in good accordance with earlier Rb-Sr dates of 36–34 Ma and zircon Sensitive High Resolution Ion Micro Probe (SHRIMP) ages of 36–35 Ma for associated igneous rocks (Zeng and others, 2006). More recent Re-Os dates have been determined on molybdenite at 35.8 Ma by Zeng and others (2006) and 35.3 Ma by Xing and others (2009).

In a study focused on the distal gold deposits (Baoxinchang, Jinchangqing) to the northeast of Machangqing, Huang and others (1996) found a close spatial association of the gold deposits with mantle-derived lamprophyre dikes that are common in the area. Bi and others (2006) studied the mineral chemistry of the intrusive rocks at Machangqing and concluded that the stocks crystallized near 730° C at a pressure of 2.2 to 2.8 kilobars (kbar) under relatively oxidizing conditions.

Prospects, Mineral Occurrences, and Related Deposit Types

Information was collected on eight porphyry copper prospects within the tract. Some of the prospects are described without coordinates or detailed maps and these are very approximately located. In addition to these eight, there is another poorly-documented mineral deposit in Vietnam that could possibly be a porphyry copper system. The prospects are listed in table B3.

The Beiya iron-gold district, about 160 km southwest of the Xifanping deposit, near the town of Dali, contains two poorly explored porphyry copper prospects associated with the Wangdongshan and Hongnitang stocks (Xu and others, 2007). These prospects are related to quartz-albite and quartz-K-feldspar porphyry stocks, and have typical grades of 0.1 to 5 percent copper and 0.03 to 3.3 g/t gold. The K-feldspar porphyries have Ar-Ar ages of about 33–25 Ma. Exploration in the district has so far focused on the gold deposits, which are being exploited, and the porphyry copper deposits remain relatively unexplored (Yang, 2010).

We found information about a porphyry copper prospect called Xiaolongtan, which is in Binchuan County, a few tens of km north of Machangqing, but few details are available and the deposit is not shown on figure B1 because it cannot be accurately located (Zhang and others, 2009; Wang and others, 2008).

Liufang is mentioned only by Yan and others (2007). They give few details, but describe it as small (14,000 t contained copper), and with a grade (1.57 percent Cu) that is more typical of skarn deposits.

Habo is a copper-gold-molybdenum porphyry prospect in the southern part of the tract that is being explored by Asia Now Resources Corporation (fig. B2). Progress there is documented on the company's website (Asia Now Resources, 2010). The deposit is at least 2,300 m by 1,600 m, and is typified by extensive potassic alteration and a quartz-magnetite-sulfide stockwork. Sampling in adits driven into the mineralized body have revealed multi-element mineralization; for example Tunnel PD11, sampled over a 100 m length, showed: Cu, 0.07 to 1.33 percent; Mo, 0.01 to 0.32 percent; and gold, 0.04 to 0.15 g/t. As of February 2011, eleven drill holes have been completed, and exploration is ongoing.

The deposit at Habo is also described by White and others (2007) and Harris and others (2007). The source rocks are described as highly oxidized granitoid rocks that have been strongly potassically altered, including the development of

Table B3.   Significant prospects and occurrences in tract 142pCu8711, Dali—China and Vietnam.

[Ma, million years; Mt, million metric tons; n.d., no data; %, percent; FeOX, iron oxide-rich; Cu, copper; Mo, molybdenum; Au, gold; kt, thousand metric tons; t, metric tons; g/t, grams per metric ton]

Name	Latitude	Longitude	Age (Ma)	Comments (grade and tonnage data, if available)	Reference
Wangdongshan/ Hongnitang	26.16	100.19	29	Appears to be Au-rich	Xu and others (2007)
Xiaolongtan	25.6	100.5	Oligocene	Location very approximate	Zhang and others (2009), Wang and others (2008)
Liufang	23.38	102.39	Cenozoic	Unsubstantiated resource estimate of 14,000 t Cu; may be a skarn deposit	Yan and others (2007)
Habo	22.88	102.54	37	Under active exploration; quartz-magnetite-sulfide stockwork	Asia Now Resources (2010), White and others (2007), Harris and others (2007)
Tongchang	22.80	103.04	34	Also called Chang'an; estimated grades of 1.5% Cu, 0.12% Mo, and 6 g/t Au; may be a skarn deposit	Wang and others (2005), Hou and others (2006)
Changpingchong	22.77	103.01	Cenozoic	Unsubstantiated resource estimate of 30,000 t Cu; may be a skarn deposit	Yan and others (2007)
Minle	n.d.	n.d.	presumed Cenozoic	Exact location unknown; west of Habo	Li (2000)
Xionglumo	n.d.	n.d.	presumed Cenozoic	Exact location unknown; near Machanqing	He and others (2004)
Sin Quyen	22.60	103.83	Tertiary	May be FeOX-Cu-Au or Cu-Au skarn. Contains at least 500 Kt Cu.	McLean (2002)

abundant secondary K-feldspar and biotite. These rocks were previously described as syenites because their hydrothermal alteration was not recognized. Biotite-feldspar porphyry has SiO_2 contents between 52 and 62 percent; quartz-feldspar porphyry is 67 to 73 percent SiO_2 (Zhu and others, 2009). Zircons from these rocks yield U-Pb ages of about 36 Ma; an unpublished Rb-Sr model age is 37.3 Ma. Molybdenite from the deposit is dated at about 35.5 Ma by the Re-Os method.

Tongchang was identified as a porphyry copper prospect by Wang and others (2005) and Hou and others (2006) (who referred to it as Chang'an). Wang and others (2005) determined a Re-Os age on molybdenite of 34.4 Ma, similar to earlier Rb-Sr ages that range from 36 to 34 Ma. No papers include a description of the deposit, but Hou and others (2006) suggest grades of 1.5 percent copper, 0.12 percent molybdenum, and 6 g/t gold and report that it consists of veinlets disseminated in syenites and granite host rocks.

Changpingchong is mentioned only by Yan and others (2007). They give few details, but describe it as small (30,000 t contained copper), with a grade (1.48 percent Cu) that is more typical of skarn deposits. Changpingchong and Tongchang (Chang'an) may be different names for the same deposit.

About 75 km to the southeast, just across the border in Vietnam, the Sin Quyen deposit has been classified as a Fe oxide-Cu-Au-REE deposit (McLean, 2002), however very little has been published about the deposit and its classification is uncertain; it could be a copper-gold skarn. Although it is in production it is treated here as a prospect because of the uncertainty in classification and lack of tonnage and grade

information. It is one of the larger copper deposits in southeast Asia, containing at least 500,000 t of copper (McLean, 2002).

Some information was found regarding three other deposits in southernmost Yunnan that are referred to as porphyry copper or copper-polymetallic deposits. They are Xionglumo (near Machangqing; He and others, 2004) Minle (west of Habo; Li, 2000), and Puerdi (Yang, 2009). It was not possible to determine a location for these deposits.

Figure B2.   View of Habo prospect, showing exploration tunnels in middleground.

In addition to these porphyry copper prospects, a number of recently discovered hydrothermal gold deposits related to alkaline intrusive rocks within the tract have been described as porphyry gold deposits (Bi and others, 2004). These deposits may be distal expressions of porphyry copper-gold systems. Many of the deposits and prospects in the tract, including Xifanping and Machangqing, are most closely related to late quartz-saturated rocks (granite and quartz monzonite) but alkaline rocks (syenite and alkaline lamprophyre) are important parts of the igneous assemblage. The alkaline rock association and widespread occurrence of porphyry gold deposits and gold- and iron-rich skarns in the tract (Xu and others, 2007) are reminiscent of the assemblage of igneous rocks and ore deposits in the southern Rocky Mountains, USA, described by Kelley and Ludington (2002) and termed Great Plains Margin deposits by McLemore (1996). In contrast to the Dali tract, the tectonic setting in the southern Rocky Mountains has been considered to be back-arc extensional and there are no prominent shear zones.

Exploration History

Exploration for porphyry copper deposits in this tract is at a relatively early stage, as the porphyry copper model was not well-known in China until the 1960s, when scientific and industrial activity was renewed after a long period of warfare and internal turmoil. Since that time, basic geologic mapping, as well as detailed geochemical and geophysical surveys have been completed, resulting in the discovery of several of the presently known prospects, including Xifanping and Machangqing. Nevertheless, the discovery of the Habo system in 2005, due to heavy rainfall that revealed previously hidden outcrops, demonstrates that discoveries based on modern understanding of porphyry systems are still likely (White and others, 2007). Most of the tract is variably populated, but terrain is steep, and vegetative cover hampers exploration. The current level of exploration activity in this tract is not well known, however, the presence of Asia Now Resources at the Habo project shows that non-Chinese exploration companies are exploring for porphyry copper deposits in this part of China.

Stream-sediment geochemical surveys conducted by the China Geological Survey have been instrumental in the discovery of many of the deposits and prospects in western China. A nationwide geochemical map for copper (China Geological Survey, 2010b) shows prominent anomalies near both Xifanping and Machangqing, but the widespread occurrence of copper-rich basalts of the Emeishan basalt province confounds the use of stream-sediment data for exploration for porphyry deposits in this part of China.

Sources of Information

Principal sources of information used by the assessment team for delineation of the tract are listed in table B4. No geophysical data at an appropriate scale were available for the assessment.

Grade and Tonnage Model Selection

Both known porphyry copper deposits in the tract have gold grades in excess of 0.3 g/t and qualify as porphyry Cu-Au deposits. In addition, there are numerous gold deposits in the tract that are related to the same suite of alkaline igneous rocks as the porphyry copper deposits. High gold grades have also been reported from several of the prospects in the tract. For all the reasons above, the gold-rich porphyry copper grade and tonnage model was judged to be the most appropriate model, and was used for the estimation of undiscovered resources in the Dali tract.

Estimate of the Number of Undiscovered Deposits

Rationale for the Estimate

Two known deposits and at least eight porphyry copper prospects have been identified in the Dali tract. Wang and others (2005) state that "a lot of Cu-Au deposits and occurrences related to syenite porphyry have been discovered recently" in the tract. Much of the area is extremely rugged and access is difficult. Continued exploration in this area is likely to result in the discovery of additional porphyry copper deposits.

Based in part on the presence of at least eight prospects in a productive area, the team estimated that there was a 90 percent chance of two or more undiscovered deposits in the tract; we believe that several of the presently identified prospects will, upon thorough exploration and development, become deposits. The relatively small size of the tract limits the total number of undiscovered deposits that might exist there, and the team estimated only 18 undiscovered deposits at the 10th percentile confidence level. The estimated mean number of undiscovered deposits is 8.3 (table B5).

Because tract delineation is a subjective process, it could be misleading to place great credence in a calculated deposit density for this tract, but the assessment team's estimate is entirely consistent with worldwide deposit density estimates (Singer, 2008; Singer and others, 2005).

A previous assessment (Yan and others, 2007) covered much of the tract (their Tract XI-4c and part of tract XI). They estimated about 4 mean undiscovered deposits, compared with the present team's estimate of 8.3 (table B5). The results of exploration conducted in the years since the earlier estimate was made can explain much of the difference. Combined with the 2 known deposits, the tract probably contains about 10 porphyry copper deposits.

Probabilistic Assessment Simulation Results

Undiscovered resources for the tract were estimated by combining the team's estimate for numbers of undiscovered porphyry copper deposits with the porphyry copper-gold model of Singer and others (2008) using the EMINERS program

Table B4.   Principal sources of information used for tract 142pCu8711, Dali—China and Vietnam.

[NA, not applicable]

Theme	Name or Title	Scale	Citation
Geology	Regional geology of Sichuan Province	1:1,000,000	Bureau of Geology and Mineral Resources of the Sichuan Province (1991)
	Regional geology of Yunnan Province	1:1,000,000	Bureau of Geology and Mineral Resources of the Yunnan Province (1990)
	Potassic magmatism in Western Sichuan and Yunnan Provinces, SE Tibet, China—Constraints on petrogenesis	NA	Guo and others (2005)
	Porphyry Cu-Au and associated polymetallic Fe-Cu-Au deposits in the Beiya Area, western Yunnan Province, south China	NA	Xu and others (2007)
Mineral occurrences	Porphyry copper deposits of the world: database, map, and grade and tonnage models	NA	Singer and others (2008)
	Metal Mining Agency of Japan mineral deposit database	NA	Metal Mining Agency of Japan (1998)
	World minerals geoscience database	NA	Natural Resources Canada (2010); Kirkham and Dunne (2000)
	Geological Survey of Japan mineral resources map of East Asia	NA	Kamitani and others (2007)
Stream-sediment geochemistry	Copper geochemical map	1: 12,000,000	China Geological Survey (2010b)
	Bismuth geochemical map	1: 12,000,000	China Geological Survey (2010a)

Table B5.   Undiscovered deposit estimates, deposit numbers, tract area, and deposit density for tract 142pCu8711, Dali—China.

[N_{xx}, estimated number of deposits associated with the xxth percentile; N_{und}, expected number of undiscovered deposits; s, standard deviation; $C_v\%$, coefficient of variance; N_{known}, number of known deposits in the tract that are included in the grade and tonnage model; N_{total}, total of expected number of deposits plus known deposits; area, area of permissive tract in square kilometers; density, deposit density reported as the total number of deposits per km^2. N_{und}, s, and $C_v\%$ are calculated using a regression equation (Singer and Menzie, 2005)]

Consensus undiscovered deposit estimates					Summary statistics					Tract area (km^2)	Deposit density (N_{total}/km^2)
N_{90}	N_{50}	N_{10}	N_{05}	N_{01}	N_{und}	s	$C_v\%$	N_{known}	N_{total}		
2	6	18	18	18	8.3	5.9	72	2	10	96,670	0.00011

Table B6.   Results of Monte Carlo simulations of undiscovered resources for tract 142pCu8711, Dali—China and Vietnam.

[Cu, copper; Mo, molybdenum; Au, gold; and Ag, silver; in metric tons; Rock, in million metric tons]

Material	Probability of at least the indicated amount						Probability of	
	0.95	0.9	0.5	0.1	0.05	Mean	Mean or greater	None
Cu (t)	200,000	1,300,000	15,000,000	64,000,000	87,000,000	26,000,000	0.36	0.04
Mo (t)	0	0	54,000	470,000	670,000	150,000	0.28	0.16
Au (t)	24	130	1,200	4,600	5,900	1,900	0.38	0.04
Ag (t)	0	0	3,100	24,000	42,000	8,600	0.25	0.11
Rock (Mt)	56	320	3,300	13,000	16,000	5,200	0.37	0.04

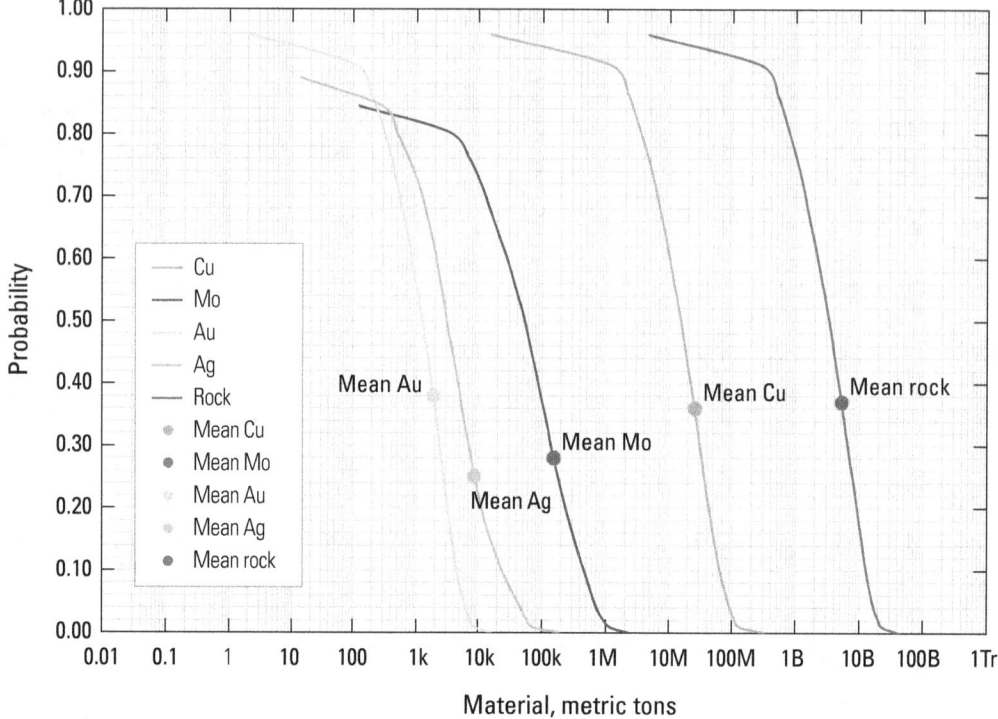

Figure B3. Cumulative frequency plot showing the results of Monte Carlo computer simulation of undiscovered resources for tract 142pCu8711, Dali—China. k, thousand; M, million; B, billion; Tr, trillion.

(Root and others, 1992; Bawiec and Spanski, 2012; Duval, 2012). Selected simulation results are reported in table B6. Results of the Monte Carlo simulation are presented as a cumulative frequency plot (fig. B2), which shows the estimated resource amounts associated with cumulative probabilities of occurrence, as well as the mean, for each commodity and for total mineralized rock.

References Cited

Asia Now Resources, 2010, Habo project: report, accessed October 14, 2010, at http://www.asianow.ca/s/Habo.asp.

Bawiec, W.J., and Spanski, G.T., 2012, Quick-start guide for version 3.0 of EMINERS—Economic Mineral Resource Simulator: U.S. Geological Survey Open-File Report 2009–1057, 26 p., accessed June 30, 2012, at http://pubs.usgs.gov/of/2009/1057. (This report supplements USGS OFR 2004–1344.)

Bi, Xianwu, Hu, Ruizhong, and Cornell, D.H., 2004, The alkaline porphyry associated Yao'an gold deposit, Yunnan, China—Rare earth element and stable isotope evidence for magmatic-hydrothermal ore formation: Mineralium Deposita, v. 39, p. 21–30.

Bi, Xianwu, Hu, Ruizhong, Mungall, J.E., Hanley, J.J., Peng, Jiantang, Wu, Kaixing, and Li, Hongli, 2006, Mineral chemistry studies of Cu- and Au-mineralized alkaline intrusions: Acta Mineralogica Sinica, v. 26, p. 377–386. [In Chinese, with English abstract.]

Bonham-Carter, G.F., Agterberg, F.P., and Wright, D.F., 1989, Weights of evidence modeling—A new approach to mapping mineral potential, in Agterberg, F.P. and Bonham-Carter, G.F., eds., Statistical Applications in the Earth Sciences: Geological Survey of Canada Paper 89-9, p. 171–183.

Bureau of Geology and Mineral Resources of the Sichuan Province, 1991, Regional geology of Sichuan Province—Geological Memoirs, series 1, no. 23: Geological Publishing House, Beijing, 730 p. [Includes geological maps at 1:1,000,000 scale, magmatic rock maps at 1:1,000,000 scale, metamorphic maps at 1:2,000,000 scale, and geological structure maps at 1:2,000,000 scale.]

Bureau of Geology and Mineral Resources of the Yunnan Province, 1990, Regional geology of Yunnan Province—Geological Memoirs, series 1, no. 21: Geological Publishing House, Beijing, 728 p. [Includes geological maps at 1:1,000,000 scale, magmatic maps at 1:1,000,000 scale, metamorphic maps at 1:2,000,000 scale, and geological structure maps at 1:1,000,000 scale.]

Chen, Peirong, Chen, Xiao Ming, Ni, Peri, Wang, Rucheng, Shen, Weizhou, and Xu, Shijin, 1996, Discovery of chalcopyrite daughter mineral in polyphase fluid inclusions from Yanyuan porphyry copper deposit, Sichuan Province: Chinese Science Bulletin, v. 41, p. 1281–1283.

Chen, Yongqing, Xia, Qinglin, Huang, Jingning, Chenm Jianguo, and Li, Jianguo, 2007, Application of the weights-of-evidence method in mineral resource assessments in the southern segment of the Sanjiang metallogenic zone, southwestern China: Geology in China, v. 34, p. 132–141.

China Geological Survey, 2010a, Bismuth geochemical map: accessed August 13, 2011, at http://www.ngac.cn/Gallery_New/Default.aspx?tab=last&type=image&node=9&id=966.

China Geological Survey, 2010b, Copper geochemical map: accessed August 13, 2011, at http://www.ngac.cn/Gallery_New/Default.aspx?tab=last&type=image&node=13&id=966.

Cox, D.P., 1986, Descriptive model of porphyry Cu, *in* Cox, D.P., and Singer, D.A., eds., 1986, Mineral deposit models: U.S. Geological Survey Bulletin 1693, p. 76. (Also available at http://pubs.usgs.gov/bul/b1693/.)

Deng, Wanming, Huang, Xuan, and Zhong, Dalai, 1998, Alkali-rich porphyry and its relation with intraplate deformation of north part of Jinsha River belt in western Yunnan, China: Science in China, Series D, v. 41, p. 297–305.

Duval, J.S., 2012, Version 3.0 of EMINERS—Economic Mineral Resource Simulator: U.S. Geological Survey Open-File Report 2004–1344, accessed June 30, 2012, at http://pubs.usgs.gov/of/2004/1344.

Guo, Xiadong, Wang, Zhihua, Chen, Xiang, Wang, Xin, and Wang, Shuxian, 2009, Machangqing porphyry-type Cu-Mo-Au deposit, Yunnan province—Geological characteristics and its genesis: Acta Geologica Sinica, v. 83, p. 1901–1914. [In Chinese, with English abstract.]

Guo, Xiadong, Wang, Zhihua, Wang, Xin, Chen, Xiang, Wang, Shaoming, and Qin, Wenming, 2010, Structural controls on formation of igneous and Machangqing porphyry-type copper-molybdenum polymetallic deposit: Geotectonica et Metallogenia, v. 34, p. 55–62. [In Chinese, with English abstract.]

Guo, Zhengfu, Hertogen, Jan, Liu, Jiaqi, Pasteels, Paul, Boven, Ariel, Punzalan, Lea, He, Huaiyu, Luo, Xiangjun, and Zhang, Wenhua, 2005, Potassic magmatism in western Sichuan and Yunnan Provinces, SE Tibet, China—Petrological and geochemical constraints on petrogenesis: Journal of Petrology, v. 46, p. 33–78.

Harris, C.H., White, N.C., Cooke, D.R., Allen, Charlotte, and Campbell, I.H., 2007, Fluid saturation in the Habo South porphyry Cu-Au (Mo) system, Southern China—Application of petrology to mineral exploration, *in* Andrew, C.J. and others (eds.), Digging Deeper: Dublin, Ireland, Proceedings of the Society for Geology Applied to Mineral Deposits, 20th-23rd August 2007, p. 411–414.

He, Mingqin, Liu, Jiajun, Yang, Shiyu, and Li, Chaoyang, 2004, Ore-forming fluid of Xionglumo copper polymetallic ore deposit in Binchuan, Yunnan: Acta Mineralogica Sinica, v. 24, p. 261–265. [In Chinese, with English abstract.]

Hou Zengqian, Zeng Pusheng, Geo Yongfeng, Du Andao, and Fu Deming, 2006, Himalayan Cu–Mo–Au mineralization in the eastern Indo–Asian collision zone—Constraints from Re–Os dating of molybdenite: Mineralium Deposita, v. 41, p. 33–45.

Hou, Zengqian, Zhang, Hongrui, Pan, Xiaofei, and Yang, Zhiming, 2011, Porphyry (Cu -Mo-Au) deposits related to melting of thickened mafic lower crust—Examples from the eastern Tethyan metallogenic domain: Ore Geology Reviews, v. 39, p. 21–45.

Hou, Zenqian, Zhong, Dalai, Deng, Wanming, and Zaw, Khin, 2005, A tectonic model for porphyry copper-molybdenum-gold deposits in the eastern Indo-Asian collision zone, *in* Porter, T.M., ed., Super porphyry copper and gold deposits—A global perspective: Adelaide, PGC Publishing, v. 2, p. 423–440.

Hou, Zengquian, Tian, Shihong, Xie, Yuling, Yang, Zhusen, Yuan, Zhongxin, Yin, Shuping, Yi, Longsheng, Fei, Hongcai, Zou, Tianren, Bai, Ge, and Li, Xiaoyu, 2009, The Himalayan Mianning-Dechang REE belt associated with carbonatite-alkaline complexes, eastern Indo-Asian collision zone, SW China: Ore Geology Reviews, v. 36, p. 65–89.

Huang, Zhilong, Wank, Liankui, and Zhu, Chengming, 1996, Study on geochemistry and genesis of lamprophyres in Machangqing gold deposits area, Yunnan province: Journal of Mineralogy and Petrology, v. 16, p. 82–89. [In Chinese, with English abstract.]

John, D.A., Ayuso, R.A., Barton, M.D., Blakeley, R.J., Bodnar, R.J., Dilles, J.H., Gray, F., Graybeal, F.T., Mars, J.C., McPhee, D.K., Seal, R.R., Taylor, R.D., and Vikre, P.G., 2010, Porphyry copper deposit model, chap. B of Mineral deposit models for resource assessment: U.S. Geological Survey Scientific Investigations Report 2010-5070-B, 169 p.

Kamitani, M., Okumura, K., Teraoka, Y., Miyano, S., and Watanabe, Y., 2007, Mineral resources map of East Asia: Geological Survey of Japan, data sheet and explanatory notes, accessed February 8, 2010, at http://www.gsj.jp/Map/EN/docs/overseas_doc/mrm-e_asia htm.

Kelley, K.D., and Ludington, Steve, 2002, Cripple Creek and other alkaline-related gold deposits in the southern Rocky Mountains, USA—Influence of regional tectonics: Mineralium Deposita, v. 37, p. 38–60.

Kirkham, R.V., and Dunne, K.P.E., 2000, World distribution of porphyry, porphyry-associated skarn, and bulk-tonnage epithermal deposits and occurrences: Geological Survey of Canada Open File 3792a, 26 p.

Li, Lizhu, Zhao, Zhigang, He, Jinliang, and Yang, Zexiang, 2006, Geological characteristics of Mofancun Himalahyan porphyry copper deposit in Yanyan, Sichuan Province: Mineral Deposits, v. 25, p. 269–280. [In Chinese, with English abstract.]

Li, Wenyao, 2000, The application of TEM to ore-prospecting work in the Minle porphyry copper ore district: Geophysical and Geochemical Exploration, v. 24, p. 391–393. [In Chinese, with English abstract.]

McLean, R.N., 2002, The Sin Quyen iron oxide-copper-gold-rare earth oxide mineralisation of North Vietnam, *in* Porter, T.M., ed., Hydrothermal iron oxide copper-gold and related deposits—A global perspective: Adelaide, PGC Publishing, p. 293–301.

McLemore, V.T., 1996, Great Plains Margin (alkaline-related) gold deposits in New Mexico, *in* Coyner, A.R., and Fahey, P.L., eds., Geology and ore deposits of the American Cordillera: Geological Society of Nevada Symposium Proceedings, v. 2, p. 935–950.

Metal Mining Agency of Japan (MMAJ), 1998, Mineral resources map of Asia: Metal Mining Agency of Japan, 1 sheet and 43 p.

Natural Resources Canada, 2010, World minerals geoscience database: accessed February 8, 2010, at http://gsc nrcan.gc.ca/wmgdb/index_e.php.

Peng, Z., Watanabe, M., Hoshino, K., Sueoka, S., Yano, T., and Nishido, H., 1998, The Machangqing copper-molybdenum deposits, Yunnan, China—An example of Himalayan porphyry-hosted Cu-Mo mineralization: Mineralogy and Petrology, v. 63, p. 95–117.

Root, D.H., Menzie, W.D., and Scott, W.A., 1992, Computer Monte Carlo simulation in quantitative resource estimation: Natural Resources Research, v. 1, no. 2, p. 125–138.

Singer, D.A., 2008, Mineral deposit densities for estimating mineral resources: Mathematical Geosciences, v. 40, p. 33–46.

Singer, D.A. and Menzie, W.D., 2005, Statistical guides to estimating the number of undiscovered mineral deposits—An example with porphyry copper deposits, in Cheng, Qiuming, and Bonham-Carter, Graeme, eds., Proceedings of IAMG—The annual conference of the International Association for Mathematical Geology: Toronto, Canada, Geomatics Research Laboratory, York University, p. 1028–1033.

Singer, D.A., Berger, V.I., Menzie, W.D., and Berger, B.R., 2005, Porphyry copper density: Economic Geology, v. 100, no. 3, p. 491–514.

Singer, D.A., Berger, V.I., and Moring, B.C., 2008, Porphyry copper deposits of the world: U.S. Geological Survey Open-File Report 2008–1155, 45 p., accessed August 10, 2009, at http://pubs.usgs.gov/of/2008/1155/.

U.S. Department of State, 2009, Small-scale digital international land boundaries (SSIB)—Lines, edition 10, and polygons, beta edition 1, *in* Boundaries and sovereignty encyclopedia (B.A.S.E.): U.S. Department of State, Office of the Geographer and Global Issues.

Wagner, Bianca, 2003, GIS-based analysis of Cenozoic geodynamics and mineralization history of the eastern syntaxis of the Himalayas (NW Yunnan, PR China): Ph.D. Dissertation, Georg August University of Göttingen, accessed March 23, 2011, at http://webdoc.sub.gwdg.de/diss/2004/wagner/wagner.pdf. [In German.]

Wang, Anjian, Cao, Dianhua, Guan, Ye, Liu, Junlai, and Li, Wenchang, 2009, Metallogenic belts of southern Three Rivers region, southwest China—Distribution, characteristics, and discussion: Acta Geologica Sinica, v. 83, p. 1365–1375. [In Chinese, with English abstract.]

Wang Denghong, Qu Wenjun, Li Zhiwei, Yin Hanlong, and Chen Yuchan, 2005, Mineralization episode of porphyry copper deposits in the Jinshajiang-Red River mineralization belt—Re-Os dating—Science in China Series D: Earth Sciences, v. 48, no. 2, p. 192–198.

Wang, Jiangzhen, Lu, Yan, Li, Zeqin, Su, Yan, Luo, Li, Yao, Zude, and Zhao, Zhigang, 2001a, Supergene enrichment of Xifanping porphyry copper deposit, Sichuan, China: Contributions to Geology and Mineral Resources Research, v. 16, p. 232–237. [In Chinese, with English abstract.]

Wang, Jianghai, Yin, An, Harrison, T.M., Grove, Marty, Zhang, Yuquan, and Xie, Guanghong, 2001b, A tectonic model for Cenozoic igneous activities in the eastern Indo-Asian collision zone: Earth and Planetary Science Letters, v. 188, p. 123–133.

Wang, Lie, Chen, Liang, and Sun, Deyu, 2008, Xiaolongtan porphyry Cu deposit of Binchuan, Dali: Yunnan Geology, v. 27, p. 253–256. [In Chinese, with English abstract.]

Wang, Zihua, Guo, Xiaodong, Yu, Wanqiang, Zhou, Yiling, Xu, Tao, and Zhang, Yong, 2010, Geological features and mineralization rules of the Machangqing Cu-Mo-Au multiple metallic deposit, Yunnan province: Geology and Exploration, v. 46, p. 214–223. [In Chinese, with English abstract.]

White, N.C., Yang, Kaihui, and Li, Wenchang, 2007, Discovery of the Habo porphyry Cu-Au-(Mo) system in Southern China—Its lessons for exploration everywhere, *in* Andrew, C.J. and others (eds.), Digging Deeper: Dublin, Ireland, Proceedings of the Society for Geology Applied to Mineral Deposits, 20th-23rd August 2007, p. 489–492.

Wu, Kaixing, Hu, Ruizhong, Bi, Xianwu, Peng, Jiantang, Zhan, Xinzhi, and Chen, Long, 2005, Island-arc geochemical signatures of Cenozoic alkali-rich intrusive rocks from western Yunnan and their implication: Chinese Journal of Geochemistry, v. 24, p. 361–369.

Xiao, Yuanfu, Sun, Yan, Wang, Jianzhen, Ly, Yan, and Wen, Chunqi, 1999, Petrology of Himalayan porphyries in Yanyuan, Sichuan, and their specialization for mineralization: Geology and Prospecting, v. 35, p. 37–39. [In Chinese, with English abstract.]

Xing, Junbing, Guo, Xiadong, Qu, Wenjun, Wang, Zhihua, and Li, Hanguang, 2009, Molybdenite Re-Os age and other geological meaning of Machangqing porphyry copper-molybdenum deposit: Gold Science and Technology, v. 17, p. 24–29. [In Chinese, with English abstract.]

Xu Xingwang, Cai Xinping, Xiao, Qibing, and Peters, Stephen G., 2007, Porphyry Cu–Au and associated polymetallic Fe–Cu–Au deposits in the Beiya Area, western Yunnan Province, south China: Ore Geology Reviews, v. 31, p. 224–246.

Yan, Guangsheng, Qiu, Ruizhao, Lian, Changyun, Nokleberg, Warren J., Cao, Li, Chen, Xiufa, Mao, Jingwen, Xiao, Keyan, Li, Jinyi, Xiao, Qinghui, Zhou, Su, Wang, Mingyan, Liu, Dawen, Yuan, Chunhua, Han, Jiuxi, Wang, Liangliang, Chen, Zhen, Chen, Yuming, Xie, Guiqing, and Ding, Jianhua, 2007, Quantitative assessment of the resource potential of porphyry copper systems in China: Earth Science Frontiers, v. 14, p. 27–41.

Yang, Xihui, 2010, A prospecting breakthrough of the Beiya superlarge gold deposit in Yunnan Province—A successful example of rapid evaluation in commercial exploration: Geology and Exploration, v. 46, p. 995–1000. [In Chinese, with English abstract.]

Yang, Zexiang, 2009, Geological features of the Puerdi porphyry copper deposit in Muli, Sichuan: Geology, v. 29, p. 132–135. [In Chinese, with English abstract.]

Zeng, Pusheng, Hou, Zengquian, Gao, Yongfeng, and Du, Andao, 2006, The Himalayan Cu-Mo-Au mineralization in the eastern Indo-Asian collision zone—Constraints from Re-Os dating of molybdenite: Geological Review, v. 52, p. 72–84. [In Chinese, with English abstract.]

Zhang, Jinxue, Wang, Wenchao, Lei, Yangai, and Mei, Pulian, 2009, The prospecting idea of Xiaolongtan porphyry Cu deposit in Binchuan: Yunnan Geology, v. 28, p. 409–414. [In Chinese, with English abstract.]

Zhu, Xiangping, Mo, Xuanxue, White, N.C., Zhang, Bo, Sun, Mingxiang, Wang, Shuxian, Zhao, Sili, and Yang, Yong, 2009, Geology and metallogenetic setting of the Habo porphyry Cu (Mo-Au) deposit, Yunnan: Acta Geologica Sinica, v. 83, p. 1915–1928. [In Chinese, with English abstract.]

Appendix C. Porphyry Copper Assessment for Tract 142pCu8712, Gangdese—China

By Steve Ludington[1], Jane M. Hammarstrom[2], Gilpin R. Robinson, Jr.[2], and Robert J. Miller[1], based on contributions of Yan Guangsheng[3], Mao Jingwen[4], Li Jinyi[3], Xiao Keyan[3], Qiu Ruizhao[3], Shao Jianbao[3], Shai Gangyi[3], and Du Yuliang[3]

Deposit Type Assessed: Porphyry Copper

Deposit type: Porphyry copper
Descriptive model: Porphyry copper (Cox, 1986; John and others, 2010)
Grade and tonnage model: General porphyry copper (Singer and others, 2008)
Table C1 summarizes selected assessment results.

Table C1.   Summary of selected resource assessment results for tract 142pCu8712, Gangdese—China.

[km, kilometers; km^2, square kilometers; t, metric tons]

Date of assessment	Assessment depth (km)	Tract area (km^2)	Known copper resources (t)	Mean estimate of undiscovered copper resources (t)	Median estimate of undiscovered copper resources (t)
2010	1	239,860	15,200,000	87,000,000	61,000,000

Location

The Gangdese tract extends for about 1,600 kilometers (km), from far western to far eastern Xizang Autonomous Region (Tibet) in China, just north of the Yarlung-Tsampo suture zone, which marks the boundary between the Indian and Asian continental blocks (fig. C1). Most of the tract is quite narrow, about 100 km, and much of it is in exceedingly high mountains, with elevations ranging from about 4,000 to more than 7,000 meters (m).

Geologic Feature Assessed

A belt of Late Oligocene to Miocene igneous rocks that formed in an extensional, post-subduction environment in southwest China after the collision between India and Asia.

---

[1]U.S. Geological Survey, Menlo Park, California, United States.
[2]U.S. Geological Survey, Reston, Virginia, United States.
[3]China Geological Survey, Beijing, China.
[4]Chinese Academy of Geological Sciences, Beijing, China.

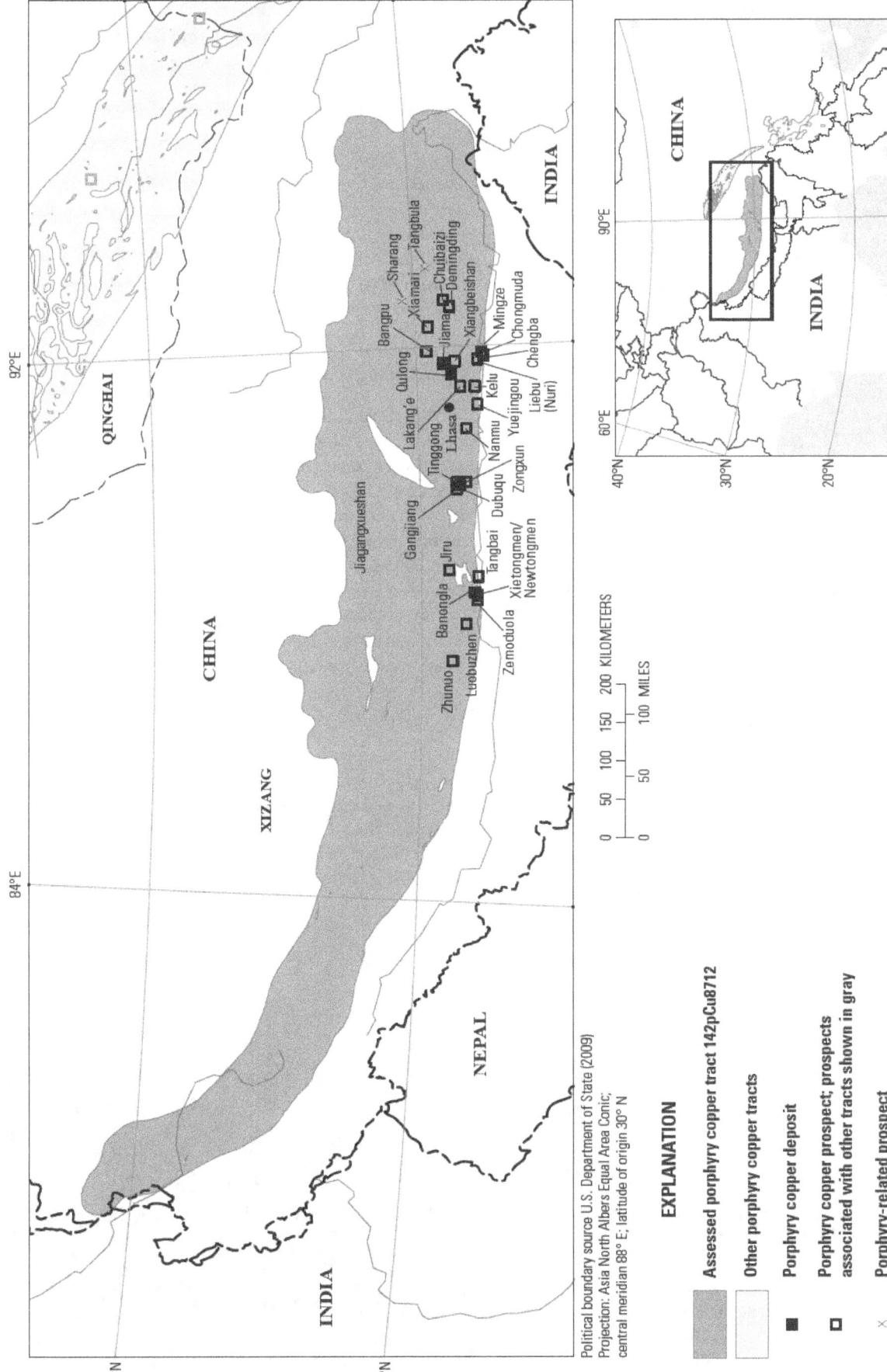

Figure C1. Map showing tract location, known porphyry copper deposits, and significant porphyry copper prospects for tract 142pCu8712, Gangdese—China.

Delineation of the Permissive Tract

Geologic Criteria

Igneous rocks that define the Gangdese tract formed during continental-scale extension and uplift during the post-collision stage of the India-Asia collision. They range in age from about 28 million years (Ma) to about 12 Ma (Qu and others, 2009), although a few may be older (Eocene). Their emplacement was guided by north-south normal faults related to rifting that accompanied rapid uplift of the Tibetan Plateau caused by continued underthrusting of the Indian continent (Qu and others, 2009; Hou and Cook, 2009; Hou and others, 2011).

The igneous rocks are mostly porphyritic intrusive rocks, though a few volcanic remnants crop out. The majority of the plutons are granodiorite, quartz monzonite, and monzogranite (Qu and others, 2007). There is an emerging consensus that they are mantle-derived melts that have assimilated important amounts of lower crustal material, as well as some upper crustal material during ascent (Hou and others, 2009; Hou and others, 2011), and that the trigger for emplacement was the uplift and extension of the Tibetan Plateau.

As a basis for tract delineation, we used an unpublished digital version of the geological map of Tibet that was published by the Chinese Ministry of Geology and Mineral Resources (Bureau of Geology and Mineral Resources of the Xizang Autonomous Region, 1993). The resulting digital geologic map does not always reflect the most recent radiometric age determinations or petrologic studies on the rocks in the tract, whose ages are not always accurately known. However, many of the rocks have not been dated precisely nor been studied extensively petrologically. In addition, many of the plutons associated with known deposits and prospects are less than a square kilometer in outcrop area, and thus are not included in the digital map.

To define the area included in the permissive tract, we first classified igneous map units as permissive or not, based on the geologic criteria described above, i.e. calc-alkaline and alkaline volcanic and plutonic rocks of Tertiary age. We then examined the more recent 1:2,500,000 scale geologic map of China (China Geological Survey, 2004) and designated units as permissive on that map as well. In addition to these polygons from the digital geologic map, we digitized additional polygons to represent those bodies shown in figure 3 of Hou and others (2009) but not present on the digital map.

We applied a 15-km buffer to plutonic rock polygons and a 2-km buffer to volcanic rock polygons. Buffering expanded the area of the tract to include deposits and prospects in the tract and accounts for uncertainties in the cartographic position of mapped boundaries, as well as possible unexposed or unmapped permissive rocks.

After initial delineation, we examined the limited available geophysical and geochemical information to be sure we included any other evidence of unmapped permissive rocks or hydrothermal systems at shallow depths. Because of the strong structural control of deposits in this tract, we also

filled any gaps in the resulting tract, to emphasize the east-west nature of the belt of mineralized intrusions. A smoothing routine was applied to the resulting polygons, and the tract was trimmed to terrane-bounding faults.

The resource assessment reported by She and others (2009) includes a map of the prospective areas they identified using a method that combined weighted geological and geochemical evidence layers. We extended the Gangdese tract in a few areas to include these prospective areas. We also excluded areas where Tertiary basins were judged to be deeper than 1 km by buffering inward 1 km from the margins of outcrops of post-mineral sedimentary rock and sediment. The tract is shown in figure C1.

Known Deposits

The Gangdese tract contains three known porphyry copper deposits (table C2), although only one, Qulong, meets all the criteria of Singer and others (2008) to be termed a deposit. Although both Xietongmen/Newtongmen and Jiama are large deposits and Jiama is in production, active exploration in the vicinity of each continues and their resources continue to grow; they cannot be considered to be completely delineated. Nevertheless, for the purposes of this assessment and because of their size, we considered both Xietongmen/Newtongmen and Jiama to be known deposits. Qulong clearly contains unexplored resources at depth, but exploration has ceased, and the deposit is being readied for production.

Xietongmen/Newtongmen Area

Xietongmen is the first porphyry copper deposit in China to be drilled out and readied for production according to western standards. About 250 km west of Lhasa, the capital, the deposit (fig. C2) was discovered by the Tibet Geological Bureau in 2000, while following up on stream-sediment geochemical anomalies. Short adits were driven in 2001 and

Figure C2.   Photograph of the Xietongmen porphyry copper deposit, Xizang (Tibet), China. Photo looking south across Yarlung-Tsangpo River, shows drill roads at an early stage of exploration.

Table C2. Porphyry copper deposits in tract 142pCu8712, Gangdese—China.

[Ma, million years; Mt, million metric tons; t, metric ton; g/t, gram per metric ton; %, percent; Cu-Mo subtype, deposits that have Au/Mo ratios <3 or average Mo grades >0.03 percent; Cu-Au subtype, deposits that have Au/Mo ratios > 30 or average Au grades >0.2 g/t, NA, not applicable. Contained Cu in metric tons is computed as tonnage (Mt × 1,000,000) × Cu grade (percent)]

Name	Latitude	Longitude	Subtype	Age (Ma)	Tonnage (Mt)	Cu (%)	Mo (%)	Au (g/t)	Ag (g/t)	Contained Cu (t)	Reference
Xietongmen/ Newtongmen	29.384	88.407	NA	not resolved	1,085	0.30	n.d.	0.22	1.20	3,310,000	Rebagliati and others (2009)
Qulong	29.625	91.594	Cu-Mo	16	1,778	0.45	0.045	n.d.	3.9	8,000,000	Hou and Cook (2009), Yang and others (2009)
Jiama	29.703	91.765	NA	15.2	1,006	0.39	0.046	0.095	5.6	3,920,000	China Gold International (2010), Tang and others (2010)

2002 and the first drilling was conducted in 2003. Between 2004 and 2011, the deposit was explored and developed by Continental Minerals Corporation of Vancouver, British Columbia. In late 2010, an agreement was announced wherein the deposit was to be purchased by Jinchuan Group Ltd. (Continental Minerals Corporation, 2010a); the arrangement was completed in the spring of 2011. Except where noted otherwise, the characterization of the deposit is derived from technical (43-101) reports concerning the property, one in 2007 (Rebagliati and others, 2007) and another describing activities in 2007 and 2008 (Rebagliati and others, 2009).

Current data indicate that the Xietongmen deposit contains 219,800,000 metric tons (t) of ore at 0.43 percent copper, 0.61 grams per metric ton (g/t) gold, and 3.87 g/t silver. (Continental Minerals Corporation, 2010b), including both measured and indicated resources, calculated at a cutoff grade of 0.15 percent copper. About 10 percent of the ore consists of supergene-enriched oxide facies material.

The deposit is hosted in Jurassic volcanic and intrusive rocks and consists of a coherent pod-shaped body of disseminated and veinlet mineralization that measures about 600 m north-south, 1,300 m east-west, and 320 m vertically. This body is elongate along a N60°W axis, parallel to several faults that appear have localized the mineralization (Xu and others, 2009). Hydrothermal alteration assemblages include potassic, phyllic (quartz-sericite-pyrite), and several varieties of propylitic alteration that include actinolite, chlorite, and albite (Rebagliati and others, 2009).

Centered about 2.5 km to the northwest of Xietongmen, Newtongmen is another important mineralized zone in the area. It has been extensively drilled since 2006, and is much larger, though lower grade, than Xietongmen. Alteration zones associated with the two deposits overlap, and it is likely that both are part of the same mineralized system, although Newtongmen has not been dated independently. The current provisional indicated plus inferred resource for Newtongmen is 865,300,000 t at 0.27 percent copper, 0.13 g/t gold, and 0.51 g/t silver, calculated at a cutoff grade of 0.15 percent copper (Continental Minerals Corporation, 2010b). This deposit contains nearly three times as much copper as Xietongmen, and exploration of this mineralized body is ongoing. Although the resource does not contain molybdenum, a table in Rebagliati and others (2009) suggests that molybdenum grades may range from 0.005 to 0.015 percent. The combined resource

for Xietongmen/Newtongmen is 1,085,000,000 t at 0.30 percent copper, 0.22 g/t gold, and 1.20 g/t silver, representing more than 3,000,000 t of copper.

The main orebody at Newtongmen is made up of quartz-pyrite-chalcopyrite-molybdenite-biotite veins and veinlets that occur primarily in potassically altered rock (biotite-magnetite-quartz-K-feldspar); mineralization is less well developed in the phyllically altered rock, which overprints some areas of potassic alteration. Propylitic alteration is only sporadically developed and may be related to post-mineralization faulting (Rebagliati and others, 2009).

The age of the Xietongmen/Newtongmen deposit is uncertain. Jurassic igneous rocks interpreted to be directly related to the deposit were dated at 174 to 171 Ma by Tafti and others (2009) using U-Pb methods on zircons. They also determined a Re-Os date on molybdenite from disseminated mineralization in drill core of 174 Ma. In contrast, two independent Ar-Ar age determinations on sericite from apparently ore-related hydrothermal alteration are late Eocene (38.1 Ma–Xu and others, 2009; 38.7 Ma–Rui and others, 2005). The situation is further complicated by an Eocene granodiorite pluton immediately to the northeast of the deposit that yielded a U-Pb zircon age of about 48 Ma (Tafti and others, 2009).

Although the deposits in the Xietongmen area may actually be Jurassic in age (145 to 200 Ma), we chose to include them in this assessment, primarily because of their location and because they are commonly referred to as part of the Gangdese porphyry belt in the Chinese literature. Other studies (see Wen and others, 2008; Ji and others, 2009) have found only a few other Jurassic rocks in the southern Lhasa terrane.

Other prospects nearby include Zemoduola, Banongla, and Tangbai (see next section).

Qulong

Qulong, located about 40 km east of the capital, Lhasa, is the largest deposit in the tract. Unless otherwise referenced, all data in this description are derived from a comprehensive study of the deposit by Yang and others (2009). Mineralized rock at the site of Qulong was first noted as early as 1986, but it was not recognized as a porphyry copper deposit until 1994. Initial drilling was in 2002, when more than 400 m of >0.5 percent copper was encountered. The property has been explored since 2006 by the

Xizang Zhongsheng Mineral Resources Company, and more than 80,000 m of drilling to depths of 850 m have been completed; the deposit is apparently being prepared for production.

Singer and others (2008) provide a resource number of 1,517,000,000 t at 0.52 percent copper, 0.03 percent molybdenum and 3.9 g/t silver. These data indicate a total copper resource of about 7,900,000 t, but unverified press reports indicate a total resource closer to 10,000,000 t of copper. Assay cross-sections published as figure 17 in Yang and others (2009) suggest the deposit is much larger, because the zone where copper is greater than 0.6 percent is about 400 m wide at the limit of drilling (about 800 m), and the zone where copper is greater than 0.3 percent is nearly 1.5 km wide at the same depth.

The deposit crops out on the surface, and is associated with a Miocene intrusion, termed the P porphyry, which has an outcrop area of about 0.2 km². This 17.6 Ma porphyry intrudes an earlier intrusion, the 19.5 Ma Rongmucuola pluton. Country rocks also include several Jurassic granitoid bodies and Jurassic volcanic rocks. Molybdenite from the ore zone has been dated by the Re-Os method at 16.4 Ma (Meng and others, 2003a) and 16.0 Ma (Rui and others, 2003).

Hydrothermal alteration assemblages displayed at Qulong are typical of those associated with other porphyry copper deposits. The core zone exhibits potassic alteration that includes K-feldspar, biotite, and anhydrite. A widespread surrounding zone of propylitic alteration includes chlorite and epidote. Both these alteration assemblages are overprinted by widespread feldspar-destructive alteration, both phyllic (quartz-sericite pyrite) and argillic (clay minerals). Daughter minerals in fluid inclusions from veinlet quartz at Qulong contain a complex assemblage including chalcopyrite and several unidentified copper-bearing minerals, in addition to the expected halite and sylvite (Yang and others, 2006).

Other deposits and prospects in the immediate area include Jiama, Lakang'e, and Xiangbeishan (see below and next section).

Jiama

Most of the ore at the Jiama deposit, about 15 km northeast of Qulong, is best termed skarn and hornfels. Information about Jiama, except when otherwise referenced, is derived from Deng and others (2009). There was small-scale lead mining at the site before the 1950s, and initial exploration by the Chinese government prior to 1990 delineated a 3.6-km-long mineralized zone. During 1991 through 1999, the Tibet Geological and Mineral Resource Bureau continued exploration, completing 31 diamond drill holes with a total drilled length of 10,091 m, and excavating several short adits and some surface trenches. Subsequently, four separate mining licenses were issued and four small-scale mining operations were active until 2007. At that time, the Tibetan government stopped mining and consolidated the mining and exploration licenses under a complex joint venture in which China Gold International Resources Corporation Ltd., a Hong Kong company, has the major interest. Since then, nearly 300 diamond drill holes with a total drilled length of more than 110 km have been completed. Mining commenced in July of 2010, with plans to expand capacity soon.

As of June 30, 2010, the combined resource (measured, indicated, and inferred) for the skarn ore body and the hornfels ore body was 1,006,000,000 t of ore at 0.39 percent copper, 0.046 percent molybdenum, 0.095 g/t gold, and 5.6 g/t silver at a cutoff grade of 0.3 percent copper or 0.03 percent molybdenum. This indicates a total copper resource of about 3,900,000 t. Moreover, the most recent drilling has encountered a "grano-porphyry type copper-molybdenum" mineralized body that appears to underlie the skarn deposit (China Gold International, 2010), and Jiama will almost certainly expand. A sophisticated remote sensing study demonstrated that hydrothermal alteration extends well beyond the explored part of the district (Guo and others, 2010).

The skarn orebody forms a thin stratiform layer that approximately follows the contact between Jurassic marble and overlying Cretaceous clastic rocks. Thickness of this layer ranges from about 2 to 240 m, and it is at least 2,400 m long along the strike direction, and 190 to 1,900 m wide downdip. Skarn mineralization consists of variable amounts of chalcopyrite, bornite, molybdenite, galena, sphalerite, and pyrite in a silicate gangue of garnet, diopside, plagioclase, wollastonite, K-feldspar, and quartz. Less abundant minerals include chalcocite, enargite, tetrahedrite, covellite, electrum, malachite, silver, and cobaltite. A much larger volume of lower-grade hornfels in the Cretaceous clastic rocks above the skarn contain much the same sulfide mineral assemblage in fractures.

A sequence of dikes composed of diorite, quartz diorite, granodiorite porphyry monzogranite porphyry, and granite porphyry are found throughout the orebodies (Tang and others, 2010). These dikes have high-K calc-alkaline compositions, and their silica contents range from about 60 to 73 percent. The have compositions similar to other igneous rocks in the Gangdese belt, characterized by relatively low abundances of niobium, tantalum, and yttrium, and relatively high barium and strontium. Four zircon U-Pb ages from these dikes range from 16.3 to 14.8 Ma. A Re-Os date on molybdenite from the deposit suggests mineralization at about 15.2 Ma, which matches the age found by Ying and others (2010) with a 27-sample Re-Os isochron.

A study of fluid inclusions at Jiama found evidence for supercritical saline fluids at temperatures up to 500° C that have hydrogen and oxygen isotope signatures typical of fluids of magmatic origin (Li and others, 2011b). The inclusions also contained methane, ethane, and propane, suggesting that the deposit formed in a relatively reducing environment.

Prospects, Mineral Occurrences, and Related Deposit Types

The tract contains more than 20 porphyry copper prospects (table C3).

Zhunuo

Zhunuo was discovered in 2004 through the reprocessing of regional geochemical data (Zheng and others, 2006), and is the westernmost identified porphyry copper system in the Gangdese tract. Results from five drill holes and sampling in two tunnels in one of three mineralized areas indicate a resource of about 1,000,000 t of copper grading 0.83 percent copper and 340 t of silver

Table C3. Significant prospects and occurrences tract 142pCu8712, Gangdese—China.

[Ma, million years; Mt, million metric tons; t, metric ton; g/t, gram per metric ton; %, percent]

Name	Latitude	Longitude	Age (Ma)	Comments	Reference
Zhunuo	29.66	87.47	13.7	Conceptual resource estimate of 120 Mt at 0.83% Cu, 0.3 g/t Au, 2.65 g/t Ag.	Zheng and others (2007a), Zheng and others (2007c)
Luobuzhen	29.50	88.00	Miocene?	Location very approximate	Chen and others (2008)
Zemoduola	29.38	88.35	unknown	Xietongmen area; few details; location from Fig. 2 of Xu and others (2009); may be Jurassic	Xu and others (2009)
Banongla	29.40	88.45	unknown	Xietongmen area; few details; location from Fig. 2 of Xu and others (2009); may be Jurassic	Xu and others (2009)
Tangbai	29.36	88.69	unknown	Xietongmen area; few details; location from Fig. 2 of Xu and others (2009); may be Jurassic	Xu and others (2009)
Jiru	29.69	88.78	Miocene?	Drilling in 2007	Zheng and others (2007a), Zheng, Duo, Zhang, and others (2007b)
Gangjiang	29.60	89.95	14	Nimu area; provisional resource of 47 Mt at 1.1% Cu (oxide); also reported as 1 5 mt of Cu, at 0.45% Cu, 0.12 g/t Au, 5 g/t Ag	Central China Goldfields (2008), Hou and Cook (2009)
Dubuqu	29.56	90.00	Miocene	Nimu area; raw prospect	Central China Goldfields (2008)
Tinggong	29.59	90.05	15.5	Nimu area; 5 drill holes through 2007; intercepts of 0.34% Cu, 0.02% Mo; oxide copper being mined; a resource of >1 Mt of Cu at a grade of 0.5% also reported	Central China Goldfields (2008), Hou and others (2009)
Zongxun	29.49	90.05	Miocene	Nimu area; raw prospect	Central China Goldfields (2008)
Nanmu	29.47	90.82	14.8	Resource reported of >0.2 Mt of Cu, at a copper grade of >0.3%	Qu and others (2007), Hou and others (2004, 2009)
Yuejingou	29.33	91.16	Oligocene?	Kelu-Chongmuda skarn belt; Cu skarn deposit	Wang (2010)
Kelu	29.36	91.41	Oligocene?	Kelu-Chongmuda skarn belt; Cu-Au skarn deposit	Li and others (2005)
Lakang'e	29.58	91.48	13.6	Limited information	Qu and others (2007), Hou and others (2004)
Xiangbeishan	29.58	91.78	Miocene?	Porphyry and skarn-type mineralization	Zheng and others (2007a), Rui and others (2005)
Liebu (Nuri)	29.32	91.80	23	Kelu-Chongmuda skarn belt; Porphyry-style mineralization below Cu-Ag skarn deposit; limited drilling	Li and others (2006)
Mingze	29.25	91.86	Oligocene to early Miocene?	Porphyry-style mineralization below Cu-Mo veins; limited drilling	Li and others (2006)
Chengba	29.25	91.87	Oligocene to early Miocene?	Kelu-Chongmuda skarn belt; Cu-Au skarn deposit	Li and others (2006)
Chongmuda	29.27	91.91	21.4	Kelu-Chongmuda skarn belt; Skarn deposit, cross-cut by porphyry-style veins	Zheng and others (2007a), Li and others (2005), Beaudoin and others (2005)
Bangpu	29.91	91.97	15.3	Kelu-Chongmuda skarn belt; Polymetallic replacement deposit underlain by porphyry-style mineralization	Hou and others (2009), Meng and others (2003b)
Xiamari	29.86	92.29	Miocene?	Limited information	Rui and others (2005)
Demingding	29.61	92.58	Miocene?	Three mineralized zones; Cu grade near 0.1% but Mo grades of 0.05–0.1%	Zheng and others (2007a)
Chuibaizi	29.68	92.68	Miocene?	Five mineralized zones; limited information	Zheng and others (2007a)
Jiagangxuweshan	30.74	88.64	21.4	W-Mo-Bi vein deposit	Wang and others (2007)
Sharang	30.18	92.68	ca. 47	Large Mo porphyry related to granite	Gao and others (2010), Qin and others (2008)
Tangbula	29.91	93.07	19.9	Porphyry deposit with both Mo- and Cu-rich zones	Zhang and others (2008)

grading 2.65 g/t silver (Zheng and others, 2007a). These data indicate about 120,000,000 t of ore. The area was actively explored in 2006 and 2007 by South China Resources PLC, who made a similar resource estimate (termed conceptual) of 120,000,000 t of ore at 0.88 percent copper and 2.77 g/t silver (South China Resources, 2006). In December of 2007, South China Resources announced it was withdrawing from further negotiations on the Zhunuo Copper Project, and no more recent information is available. The property is presently controlled by Qinghai Province Geermu Zangge Kalium Fertiliser Company Limited.

Three Miocene porphyry stocks and three associated mineralized zones within those stocks and their wall rocks have been identified at Zhunuo. Ore minerals include malachite, azurite, cuprite, native copper, chalcopyrite, pyrite, and molybdenite. Alteration assemblages are zoned from a central potassic zone through phyllic and propylitic zones; most of the mineralized rock is in the phyllic zone (Zheng and others, 2007c); South China Resources, 2006). The intrusions contain complexly zoned zircons (Zheng and others, 2007c). Their rims yielded an U-Pb age of about 13.3 Ma, which was interpreted to be the age of the plutons. Inherited ages of about 63, 50, and 16 Ma were determined deeper within the zircon crystals. A Re-Os isochron age of 13.7 Ma was also determined on molybdenite from the deposit (Zheng and others, 2007c).

Based on examination of unprocessed satellite imagery, there are several other centers of hydrothermal alteration between Zhunuo and the Xietongmen area.

Xietongmen/Newtongmen Area

A number of prospects and showings, including Banongla, Zemoduola, and Tangbai, have been identified in the region surrounding the Xietongmen and Newtongmen deposits.

Zemoduola is about 7 km west of Xietongmen. Exploration is limited, but soil and rock geochemical studies suggest that it is also a center for copper and gold mineralization (Lang and others, 2007). Banongla and Tangbai are Cu-Au occurrences that are shown on a map in Xu and others (2009); they are described as similar to Xietongmen/Newtongmen, but no further details are known, as they were not actively explored by Continental Minerals.

Another copper-polymetallic deposit, Luobuzhen, is described as being near the Xietongmen area, but its location is not well established (Chen and others, 2008).

Southwest of the Newtongmen prospect, Dongga is described by Beaudoin and others (2005) as a gold- and silver-rich polymetallic vein that consists of meter-thick west-northwest-trending veins. Early in the exploration of Xietongmen, the name Dongga was erroneously applied to the porphyry copper deposit.

Jiru

Jiru was discovered in 2001, and a brief description is given by Zheng and others (2007b). The prospect is centered on a composite porphyritic granite and monzonitic granite stock. Silicification in

the core grades outward to phyllic and propylitic hydrothermal alteration zones. Ore minerals include malachite, azurite, chalcopyrite, pyrite, molybdenite, galena, and bornite. Exploration was described as ongoing drilling. Zheng and others (2007b) states that the deposit was found by reprocessing of geochemical data to enhance minor geochemical anomalies. Re-Os data (Gong and others, 2008) indicate that Jiru is Eocene in age (51–48 Ma), similar to one possible age for the nearby Xietongmen deposit.

Nimu Area

Between May 2006 and June 2009, the Nimu area was explored by Central China Goldfields, a London-based company, under the terms of a joint venture agreement with the Sichuan Bureau of Metallurgy and Geological Exploration (SBGME). In 2009, SBGME purchased Central China Goldfields' interest and the prospect is now under their control. The project area includes the Gangjiang, Tinggong, Dubuqu, and Zongcun prospects (table C3).

Gangjiang (also known as Chongjiang) was listed as a deposit by Singer and others (2008), but the resource number provided was based on only seven drill holes. The system is being actively drilled, and its limits are undefined. For the entire project, a pre-2006 resource was estimated at 600,000 t of oxide copper at grades between 1.07 and 1.1 percent copper (corresponding to about 55,000,000 t of ore), along with 236,000 t of sulfide copper at grades between 0.29 and 0.34 percent copper (corresponding to about 70,000,000 to 80,000,000 t of ore), with molybdenum grades between 0.02 and 0.08 percent (Central China Goldfields, 2006). This area was discovered in 1990 by the use of stream-sediment geochemical studies (Central China Goldfields, 2006; Zheng, Duo, Cheng, and others, 2007; Kong and others, 2007). There is a small open-cut copper mine adjacent to Tinggong, operated by SBGME.

The area is about 100 km west of Lhasa, in Nimu county. Of the seven areas of interest, four (Gangjiang, Bairong, Ronggangmeng, and Xiaoing) are distributed around the margins of a "rhyodacite" porphyry intrusion; these are represented in the database (table C3) by Gangjiang. The other three (Tinggong, Dubuqu, and Zongcun) are distal (8 to 20 km southeast) to this system, but also related to small silicic intrusions (Central China Goldfields, 2007). Li and others (2007), using $^{40}Ar/^{39}Ar$ methods, obtained dates of about 17 Ma on hornblende from a pre-ore monzogranite, about 12.5 Ma from post-ore quartz diorite, and about 14.5 Ma from post-ore granodiorite, along with alteration ages on hydrothermal sericite of about 12 Ma. Leng and others (2010) obtained zircon U-Pb dates of 14.7 Ma on a biotite quartz monzonite and 12.0 Ma on the rhyodacite.

Exploration activity was principally focused on the Gangjiang prospect, where 21 diamond drill holes were completed, 18 of which encountered significant mineralized rock (Central China Goldfields, 2008). Numerous intercepts of tens of meters at grades of 0.1 to 0.3 percent copper and 0.01 to 0.03 percent Mo were encountered in these drill holes (Central China Goldfields, 2007). Gold values as high as 0.7 g/t and silver values as high as 12 g/t were found in the same intervals. Several areas at Ganjiang contain small amounts of enriched oxide-facies copper at or near the surface, and SBGME reported a resource of 47,000,000 t of 1.1

percent copper (oxide facies). Fluid inclusion studies at Gangjiang show that the deposit exhibits a typical porphyry inclusion assemblage of early high-temperature supercritical fluids followed by lower-temperature brine coexisting with a low-salinity vapor (Xie and others, 2007). The lack of abundant propylitic alteration suggests that the deposits have been eroded to a depth of 2 to 3 km (Leng and others, 2010).

At Bairong, surface sampling found low copper contents, and no drilling was undertaken. However, a resource of 72,000,000 t at 0.29 percent copper was reported by SBGME. Initial channel sampling at Xiaqing and Ronggangmeng also encountered relatively low grade mineralization, less than 0.1 percent copper, and no drilling was undertaken (Central China Goldfields, 2008). In this assessment, these three prospects are considered to be part of the Gangjiang prospect because of proximity (table C3); the alteration envelopes of all four appear to overlap.

At Tinggong, at least 5 drill holes were completed by 2007; these encountered numerous intercepts of tens of meters with copper grades up to 0.34 percent and Mo grades up to 0.02 percent (Central China Goldfields, 2008). Yang and others (2005, 2006) studied the daughter minerals in fluid inclusions from phenocryst and veinlet quartz at Tinggong and found a complex assemblage including chalcopyrite and several unidentified copper-bearing minerals, in addition to the expected halite and sylvite. The inclusions also indicate boiling of the ore-forming fluid took place at about 360° C.

No detailed ground work was completed at the Dubuqu and Zongxun prospects, and no information is available about the exploration conducted by SBGME between 2000 and 2006.

Hydrothermal alteration is typical for porphyry copper deposits, with potassic alteration zoned outward through poorly-developed phyllic and propylitic zones. The copper-bearing rocks are found primarily in rocks that display potassic alteration (Zheng and others, 2007a).

Miocene intrusive rocks from the Nimu project area include granodiorite porphyry, monzogranite porphyry, and quartz monzonite porphyry, and silica contents range from about 65 to 71 percent (Gao and others, 2003). Both niobium and yttrium abundances are very low (<10 ppm). Initial ratios of $^{87}Sr/^{86}Sr$ range from 0.7056 to 0.7064 and ε_{Nd} values range from -2.3 to +0.9.

Qu and others (2007) determined Re-Os ages on five molybdenite samples from Gangjiang; the model ages range from 13.8 to 14.2 Ma, and an isochron age was reported as 13.99 ± 0.16 Ma. An $^{40}Ar/^{39}Ar$ isochron age of 13.45 ± 0.26 Ma was also determined for biotite from Gangjiang. In addition, Hou and others (2004) determined a Re-Os isochron age for molybdenite from Gangjiang of 14.04 Ma, whereas Li and others (2004) determined a Re-Os model age for Gangjiang of 13.88 Ma and for Tinggong of about 15 Ma.

Nanmu

Nanmu, also called Dabu, is located between the Nimu project and the Qulong-Jiama area, about 35 km southwest of the city of Lhasa. The following description is derived primarily from Qu and others (2007). The mineralized body is

irregular in form, and is mostly in cataclastic granite that hosts the Miocene porphyries. The prospect is reported to contain more than 200,000 t of copper, at grades exceeding 0.3 percent, which corresponds to less than 67,000,000 t of ore. Ore minerals include chalcocite, covellite, malachite, chalcopyrite, pyrite, molybdenite, bornite, and sphalerite. Alteration assemblages are zoned from a central potassic zone through silicic, phyllic, and propylitic zones. Fluid inclusion studies revealed a typical porphyry inclusion assemblage of early high-temperature (>500 °C) supercritical fluids followed by lower-temperature brine coexisting with a low-salinity vapor (Zhang and others, 2003).

Gao and others (2003) provide major- and trace-element analyses, along with Sr-, Nd-, and Pb-isotope data for some of the porphyries at Nanmu. Silica contents range from about 66 to 72 percent, and both Nb and Y are very low (<10 ppm). $^{87}Sr/^{86}Sr$ initial ratios range from 0.7048 to 0.7051 and ε_{Nd} values range from -3.3 to +5.5.

SHRIMP U-Pb ages on zircons from Nanmu range from about 17 to 14 Ma (Qu and others, 2009), and the age of mineralization, determined by Re-Os dating of molybdenite, is about 14.8 Ma (Hou and others, 2004, 2009; Qu and others, 2007; Li and others, 2004).

Qulong-Jiama Area

Immediately to the east of Lhasa (20–60 km), this group includes the Xiangbeishan and Lakang'e prospects in addition to the large deposits at Qulong and Jiama. Xiangbeishan, discovered in 2005, is about 10 km east of Qulong. Both porphyry and skarn-type mineralization is present and the skarn has copper grades as high as 2.3 percent (Zheng and others, 2007a). Lakang'e is about 20 km southwest of Qulong. Chemical analyses, isotopic data, and Ar-Ar ages are reported in Qu and others (2007). A Re-Os isochron age of 13.6 Ma was determined by Hou and others (2004). However no description of the mineralized rock at Lakang'e was found. Another potential porphyry copper prospect, named Qiangdui, is briefly described by Jiang and others (2006). It is described as near Lakang'e, but coordinates are not available and we could not locate this prospect.

Kelu-Chongmuda Skarn Belt

A suite of copper-gold skarn deposits (some contain molybdenum) has recently been discovered in a belt about 50 to 100 km southeast of Lhasa (Li and others, 2006; Li and others, 2005). The deposits are related to high-K calc-alkaline rocks associated with the late collisional stage that are primarily of Oligocene and Miocene age. Many of these skarn deposits exhibit associated porphyry-style mineralization in the igneous rocks, and porphyry copper deposits may be present at deeper levels beneath these deposits (Li and others, 2011a; Li and others, 2006). Li and others (2006) provide a map with 17 deposits and occurrences; the most notable are Yuejingou, Kelu, Liebu, Mingze, Chengba, and Chengmuda.

Yuejingou, the westernmost deposit in the skarn belt, is about 40 km due south of Lhasa. It is described by Wang

(2010) and Han and others (2008) as a copper-polymetallic deposit and consists of several skarn layers. Fluid inclusion studies by Wang (2010) indicate filling temperatures as high as 430° C, which is indicative of the porphyry environment.

Kelu is about 45 km southeast of Lhasa. It is described by Li and others (2005) as a medium-sized copper-gold skarn deposit.

Liebu, also known as Nuri, is located about 40 km east of Kelu. It was described in Li and others (2005) as a large copper-silver skarn deposit, with a copper resource of more than 500,000 t, based on limited drilling. A K-Ar age of about 23 Ma was determined on quartz diorite porphyry. Li, Qin, and others (2011) provided a map that illustrates a number of layered skarn bodies interlayered with granitoid dikes. Jiang and Jiang (2006) described copper and copper-molybdenum-tungsten skarn deposits with copper grades commonly between 0.4 and 0.8 percent, and suggested that porphyry copper mineralization was found below the skarns.

Mingze is on the south bank of the Yarlung-Tsangpo River and is about 10 km southeast of Liebu and 50 km southeast of the Qulong deposit. The deposit consists of a number of discrete hydrothermal veins that contain copper and molybdenum, but has evidence of porphyry molybdenum mineralization in the deeper parts of the deposit. Limited drilling has been done and no resource has been delineated (Li, Qin, and others, 2011).

Chengba is a medium-sized copper-gold skarn deposit just 1.5 km east of the Mingze deposit (Li and others, 2005).

Chongmuda is a medium-sized copper-gold skarn deposit crosscut by porphyry style quartz-chalcopyrite veins (Beaudoin and others, 2005). It is located about 45 km south of Qulong and 5 km east of the Mingze deposit, on the south bank of the Yarlung-Tsangpo River. A K-Ar age on hornblende from the associated pluton was reported to be 21.4 Ma by Li and others (2005), whereas a zircon U-Pb date on the pluton is 27.7 Ma (Mo and others, 2008). Li and others (2006) report Re-Os dates on molybdenite from the deposit that range from 41 to 37 Ma; it is implausible that this age can represent mineralization that cuts a pluton with a 28 Ma date, so the mineralization age remains in doubt.

Bangpu is variously described as a copper-polymetallic deposit (Meng and others, 2003b) and a molybdenum-copper porphyry deposit (Zhou and others, 2010). The deposit is somewhat north of most of the other porphyry deposits in the Gangdese belt, about 75 km northeast of Lhasa. Few details are available, and there is no measured resource, but Meng and others (2003b) dated molybdenite from the deposit at about 15 Ma, similar to other porphyry deposits in the Gandese belt.

Eastern Area

Located 60–100 km east of the Qulong-Jiama deposits, this group of relatively poorly-documented prospects includes Xiamari, Chuibaizi, and Demingding. Chubaizi and Demingding are well to the east of the Qulong-Jiama area, about 130 km east of Lhasa (Figure 1 of Zheng and others, 2007a). Chuibaizi is also mentioned and shown on a map by Rui and others (2005).

Chuibaizi was discovered using stream-sediment geochemistry in 1991–1996 and is related to quartz porphyry and porphyritic biotite monzogranite that intrudes Middle Jurassic rocks. Five separate mineralized zones contain chalcocite, malachite, chalcopyrite, molybdenite, pyrrhotite, pyrite, and sphalerite. Hydrothermally altered rocks contain silicic, phyllic, argillic, and propylitic assemblages (Zheng and others, 2007a).

Demingding, discovered in 2003, consists of three separate mineralized zones. Its geology is similar to that at the Chuibaizi deposit (Zheng and others, 2007a). Copper grades are relatively low (near 0.1 percent), but the molybdenum grades range between 0.05 and 0.1 percent.

Xiamari is mentioned briefly in Rui and others (2005), but no details about the prospect are available and the location is only approximate.

There are apparently more undocumented prospects in the area, because Zheng and others (2007a), after briefly describing these eastern prospects, state that "In addition, several tens of occurrences of porphyry Cu-(Au-Pb-Zn) have been recognized in the past years, indicating a great potential of mineralization in the Gangdese belt."

Related Deposits

Jiagangxueshan, Tangbula, and Sharang are three other prospects that are not porphyry copper systems, but merit mention as they may cast some light on the metallogenic development of the tract.

Jiagangxueshan is the first major discovery in the far northern part of the tract, about 160 km north of the Xietongmen area. It is a tungsten-molybdenum-bismuth polymetallic vein deposit, and has a zircon U-Pb age of about 22.2 Ma and a molybdenite Re-Os date of about 21.4 Ma (Wang and others, 2007).

Tangbula (Zhang and others, 2008) is the easternmost porphyry in the Gangdese belt and is nearly 200 km east of Lhasa. The deposit includes two distinct mineralized zones. The larger zone is composed primarily of molybdenite and quartz-molybdenite pyrite veins; surface sampling indicates grades of approximately 0.17 percent molybdenum and 0.05 percent copper. Surface sampling at the other zone indicates average grades of 0.16 percent molybdenum and 0.21 percent copper. A small copper-oxide body has reported grades of 0.01 percent molybdenum and 0.57 percent copper. U-Pb geochronology indicates that the granodiorite porphyry associated with the deposit was emplaced at about 19.9 Ma (Xia and others, 2010). The geochemical signature of the granodiorites is similar to that of the rocks associated with porphyry copper deposits in the Gangdese belt (Guo and others, 2007).

The Sharang prospect (Qin and others, 2008) appears to be a molybdenum (only) porphyry deposit, though no copper abundance data are available. The prospect is associated with a granite porphyry and hydrothermal alteration covers an area of nearly 10 km^2. The mineralized body is believed to extend to nearly 800 m depth, based

Table C4. Principal sources of information used for tract 142pCu8712, Gangdese—China.

[NA, not applicable]

Theme	Name or Title	Scale	Citation
Geology	Regional geology of Xizang (Tibet) Autonomous Region	1:500,000	Bureau of Geology and Mineral Resources of the Xizang Autonomous Region (1993)
	Geological map of the People's Republic of China	1:2,500,000	China Geological Survey (2004)
Mineral occurrences	Porphyry copper deposits of the world: database, map, and grade and tonnage models	NA	Singer and others (2008)
	Metal Mining Agency of Japan mineral deposit database	NA	Metal Mining Agency of Japan (1998)
	World minerals geoscience database	NA	Natural Resources Canada (2010), Kirkham and Dunne (2000)
	Geological Survey of Japan mineral resources map of East Asia	NA	Kamitani and others (2007)
	Predicted target areas for Gangdese copper porphyry deposits (Figure 3)	NA	She and others (2009)
Stream-sediment geochemistry	Copper geochemical map	1: 12,000,000	China Geological Survey (2010b)
	Bismuth geochemical map	1: 12,000,000	China Geological Survey (2010a)

on electrical methods. Originally suspected to be Eocene, the granite has been dated at about 47 Ma by zircon U-Pb methods (Gao and others, 2010).

Exploration History

Exploration for porphyry copper deposits in this tract is at a relatively early stage, as the porphyry copper model was not well-known in China until the 1960s, when scientific and industrial activity was renewed after a long period of warfare and internal turmoil. Subsequently, basic geologic mapping and detailed geochemical and geophysical surveys have been completed, resulting in the discovery of the numerous deposits and prospects described here. There has been extensive exploration for outcropping deposits in the eastern part of the tract, but the western part is still remote and poorly known. Most of the tract is extremely sparsely populated, and access is poor. Most of the tract is at altitudes exceeding 4,000 m and 6,000 m peaks are numerous.

The current level of exploration activity in this tract is not well known, however, with the recent buyouts of Continental Minerals and Central China Goldfields, we believe that only Chinese exploration companies are now exploring for porphyry copper deposits in this part of China.

Stream-sediment geochemical studies conducted by the China Geological Survey have been instrumental in the discovery of many of the deposits and prospects in this tract. A nationwide geochemical map for copper (China Geological Survey, 2010b) shows prominent anomalies coincident with the Xietongmen, Jiru, Nimu, Nanmu, Qulong-Jiama, Xiamari, and Chuibaizi areas. But numerous other anomalies are displayed on this map, including some in the western part

of the tract. Sophisticated modeling techniques were used to combine geochemical data for copper, molybdenum, and gold, to produce a porphyry copper prospectivity map for the eastern part of the tract (Zuo, Cheng, and Agterberg, 2009; Zuo, Cheng, Agterberg, and Xia, 2009). Aspects of this map were used to refine the boundaries of the permissive tract.

Sources of Information

Principal sources of information used by the assessment team for delineation of the tract are listed in table C4. No geophysical data at an appropriate scale were available for the assessment. Geochemical maps were available only for copper and bismuth among porphyry-related elements.

Grade and Tonnage Model Selection

The tract includes three known deposits, Xietongmen/ Newtongmen, Qulong, and Jiama. Xietongmen has a high gold grade (0.61 g/t), whereas Newtongmen's gold grade is only 0.13 g/t. Qulong has been extensively explored, but there is no information about the abundance of gold. Qulong contains substantial molybdenum, with a grade of 0.045 percent, but Xietongmen has no reported molybdenum grade. The Jiama skarn has relatively high grades for both gold and molybdenum, but nothing is known about the metal abundances in the underlying porphyry deposit. Until more grade information is known for these deposits, it is most appropriate to use the general porphyry copper model for the assessment of the Gangdese tract.

Table C5. Undiscovered deposit estimates, deposit numbers, tract area, and deposit density for tract 142pCu8712, Gangdese—China.

[N_{xx}, estimated number of deposits associated with the xxth percentile; N_{und}, expected number of undiscovered deposits; s, standard deviation; $C_v\%$, coefficient of variance; N_{known}, number of known deposits in the tract that are included in the grade and tonnage model; N_{total}, total of expected number of deposits plus known deposits; area, area of permissive tract in square kilometers; density, deposit density reported as the total number of deposits per km^2. N_{und}, s, and $C_v\%$ are calculated using a regression equation (Singer and Menzie, 2005)]

Consensus undiscovered deposit estimates					Summary statistics					Tract area (km²)	Deposit density (N_{total}/km²)
N_{90}	N_{50}	N_{10}	N_{05}	N_{01}	N_{und}	s	$C_v\%$	N_{known}	N_{total}		
9	13	50	50	50	22.3	15.7	71	3	25	239,860	0.00010

Table C6. Results of Monte Carlo simulations of undiscovered resources for tract 142pCu8712, Gangdese—China.

[Cu, copper; Mo, molybdenum; Au, gold; Ag, silver; t, metric tons; Mt, million metric tons]

Material	Probability of at least the indicated amount						Probability of	
	0.95	0.9	0.5	0.1	0.05	Mean	Mean or greater	None
Cu (t)	7,300,000	13,000,000	61,000,000	200,000,000	250,000,000	87,000,000	0.39	0.01
Mo (t)	71,000	180,000	1,400,000	5,900,000	8,200,000	2,400,000	0.34	0.02
Au (t)	130	260	1,500	4,900	6,500	2,200	0.38	0.02
Ag (t)	480	1,600	17,000	69,000	92,000	28,000	0.35	0.03
Rock (Mt)	1,700	2,900	13,000	40,000	49,000	18,000	0.41	0.01

Estimate of the Number of Undiscovered Deposits

Rationale for the Estimate

There are three known deposits and at least 23 porphyry copper prospects in the tract. Furthermore, the analysis by She and others (2009) identified 23 additional high-priority target areas in the eastern third of the tract, in addition to the prospects compiled for this study. Much of the area is extremely rugged and difficult of access, particularly the western part, where exploration has been limited. Continued exploration in this tract will likely result in numerous additional discoveries.

A nationwide geochemical map for copper (China Geological Survey, 2010b) shows prominent anomalies coincident with the Xietongmen, Jiru, Nimu, Nanmu, Qulong-Jiama, Xiamari, and Chuibaizi areas. Numerous other anomalies, not associated with known deposits or prospects, are displayed on this map, including some in the western, poorly explored part of the tract.

The presence of at least 23 prospects (and likely at least double that number) in a productive area, coupled with the poorly explored western part of the tract, led the assessment team to estimate a 90 percent chance of 9 or more undiscovered deposits in the tract. We believe that several of the

presently-identified prospects will, upon thorough exploration and development, become deposits. Six of them (Zhunuo, Bairong, Gangjiang, Tinggong, Nanmu, and Demingding) already contain measured resources based on drill data. In contrast, the relatively small size of the tract limits the total number of undiscovered deposits that might exist there, so the team estimated 50 undiscovered deposits at the 10th percentile confidence level. The estimated mean number of undiscovered deposits is 22.3 (table C5).

Because of the subjective nature of the tract delineation, it could be misleading to place great credence in a calculated deposit density for this tract, but the team's estimate is entirely consistent with worldwide deposit density estimates (Singer, 2008; Singer and others, 2005).

A previous assessment (Yan and others, 2007) covered much of the tract (their Tract XI-2 and tract XI-3). They estimated about 13 mean undiscovered deposits, compared with our estimate of 22.3 (table C5). Continued exploration success in the years since their estimate was made can explain much of the difference between the two estimates. Also, She and others (2009) conducted an independent assessment of the Gangdese ore belt and estimated more than 100,000,000 t of copper reserves (including that already discovered), which is somewhat greater than the total predicted in this study. Combined with the three known deposits, this means that the tract probably contains 25 or more porphyry copper deposits.

Probabilistic Assessment Simulation Results

Undiscovered resources for the tract were estimated by combining the team's estimate for numbers of undiscovered porphyry copper deposits with the porphyry copper-gold model of Singer and others (2008) using the EMINERS program (Root and others, 1992; Bawiec and Spanski, 2012; Duval, 2012). Selected simulation results are reported in table C6. Results of the Monte Carlo simulation are presented as a cumulative frequency plot (fig. C3), which shows the estimated resource amounts associated with cumulative probabilities of occurrence, as well as the mean, for each commodity and for total mineralized rock.

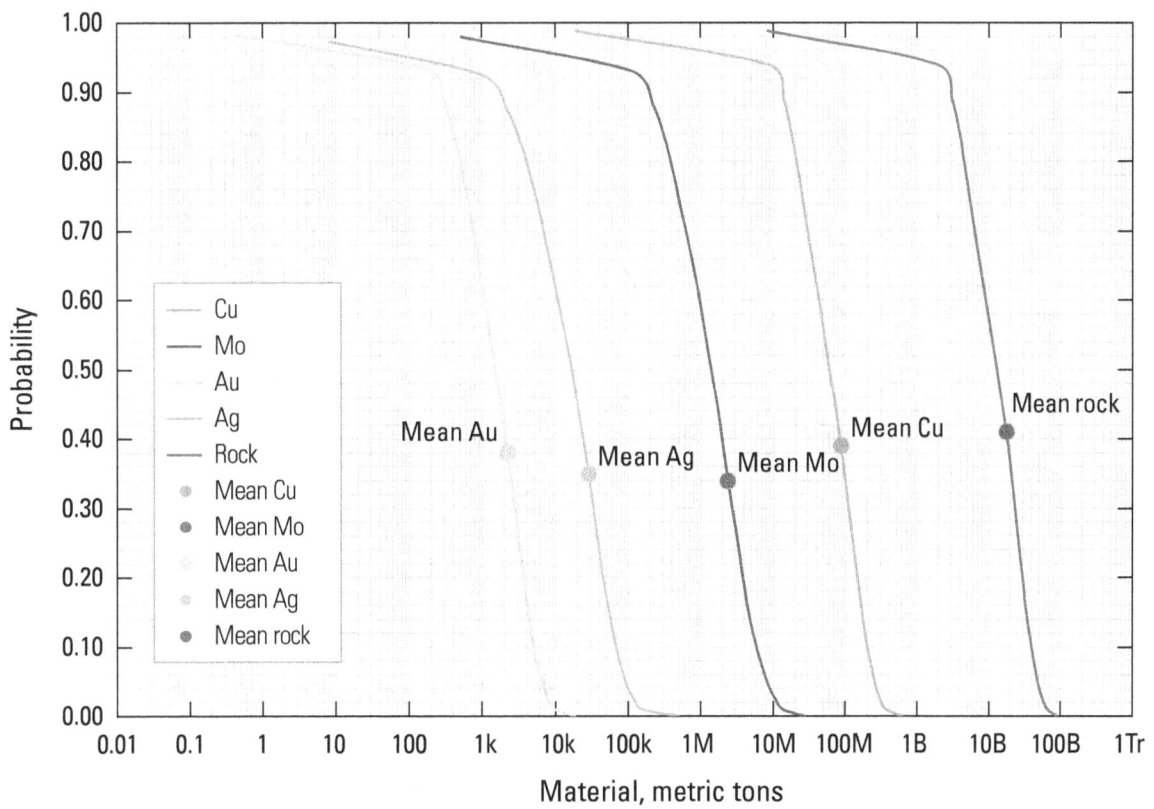

Figure C3.   Cumulative frequency plot showing results of Monte Carlo computer simulation of undiscovered resources for tract 142pCu8712, Gangdese—China. k, thousand; M, million; B, billion; Tr, trillion.

References Cited

Bawiec, W.J., and Spanski, G.T., 2012, Quick-start guide for version 3.0 of EMINERS—Economic Mineral Resource Simulator: U.S. Geological Survey Open-File Report 2009–1057, 26 p., accessed June 30, 2012, at http://pubs. usgs.gov/of/2009/1057. (This report supplements USGS OFR 2004–1344.)

Beaudoin, G., Hébert, R., Wang, C.S., and Tang, J., 2005, Epithermal Au-Ag-Cu, porphyry Cu-(Au-Mo), and Cu-Au-Ag-Zn-Pb skarn deposits of the Gangdese Arc, Tibet: Mineral Deposit Research—Meeting the Global Challenge, Proceedings of the Eighth Biennial SGA, Beijing, 2005, v. 1, p. 1219–1222.

Bureau of Geology and Mineral Resources of the Xizang Autonomous Region, 1993, Regional Geology of Xizang (Tibet) Autonomous Region: Geological Memoirs, Series 1, Number 31, Geological Publishing House, Beijing, 707 p. [Includes geological maps at 1:500,000 scale, magmatic rock maps at 1:2,000,000 scale, and tectonic maps at 1:2,000,000 scale.]

Central China Goldfields, 2006, Annual report and accounts 2006: accessed March 30, 2011, at http://www.gggresources. com/annual-report-2006.

Central China Goldfields, 2007, Annual report and accounts 2007: accessed March 30, 2011, at http://www.gggresources. com/annual-report-2007.

Central China Goldfields, 2008, Annual report and accounts 2008: accessed March 30, 2011, at http://www.gggresources. com/annual-report-2008.

Chen, Haixia, Wu, Hongli, Chen, Lingkang, Zhao, Shouren, and Jiang, Guangwu, 2008, Genesis analysis and geological characteristics of Luobuzhen copper polymetallic deposit in Xietongmen County, Tibet: Resources Environment and Engineering, v. 22, p. 401–411. [In Chinese, with English abstract.]

China Geological Survey, 2004, Geological map of the People's Republic of China: SinoMaps Press, scale 1:2,500,000, 8 sheets.

China Geological Survey, 2010a, Bismuth geochemical map: accessed August 13, 2011, at http://www.ngac.cn/Gallery_ New/Default.aspx?tab=last&type=image&node=9&id=966.

China Geological Survey, 2010b, Copper geochemical map: accessed August 13, 2011, at http://www.ngac.cn/Gallery_ New/Default.aspx?tab=last&type=image&node=13&id=966.

China Gold International, 2010, Jiama copper poly-metallic project: accessed January 2011, at http://www.chinagoldintl. com/s/Jiama.asp.

Continental Minerals Corporation, 2010a, Continental and Jinchuan Group sign formal arrangement agreement: accessed January 2011, at http://www.hdgold.com/kmk/ NewsReleases.asp?ReportID=434064&_Type=News-Releases&_Title=Continental-and-Jinchuan-Group-Sign-Formal-Arrangement-Agreement.

Continental Minerals Corporation, 2010b, Xietongmen exploration and resources: accessed January 2011, at http://www.hdgold.com/kmk/XietongmenDeposit.asp.

Cox, D.P., 1986, Descriptive model of porphyry Cu, in Cox, D.P., and Singer, D.A., eds., 1986, Mineral deposit models: U.S. Geological Survey Bulletin 1693, p. 76. (Also available at http://pubs.usgs.gov/bul/b1693/.)

Deng, Qingping, Ingham, P.D., Lepetic, V.M., and Epps, J.M., 2009, Independent technical report on the Jiama copper-polymetallic project in Metrorkongka County, Tibet Autonomous Region, the People's Republic of China: Behre Dolbear Asia Inc., 110 p., accessed January 2011, at http://www.sedar.com/GetFile.do?lang=EN&d ocClass=24&issuerNo=00016269&fileName=/csfsprod/ data110/filings/01636451/00000001/s%3A%5CSEDAR %5CTechnicalReport%5CJiama9Sept2010%5CJiamaTec hnicalReportSept92010.pdf.

Duval, J.S., 2012, Version 3.0 of EMINERS—Economic Mineral Resource Simulator: U.S. Geological Survey Open-File Report 2004–1344, accessed June 30, 2012, at http://pubs.usgs.gov/of/2004/1344.

Gao, Yiming, Chen, Yuchuan, and Tang, Juxing, 2010, SHRIMP zircon U-Pb and amphibole $^{40}Ar/^{39}Ar$ dating of amphibole diorite from Sharang porphyry molybdenum deposit in Gongbo'gyamda County, Tibet, and its geological implications: Mineral Deposits, v. 29, p. 324–331. [In Chinese, with English abstract.]

Gao, Yongfeng, Hou, Zengqian, Wei, Ruihua, and Zhao, Rongsheng, 2003, Post-collisional adakitic porphyries in Tibet—geochemical and Sr-Nd-Pb isotopic constraints on partial melting of oceanic lithosphere and crust-mantle interaction: Acta Geologica Sinica, v. 77, p. 194–203. [In Chinese, with English abstract.]

Gong, Fuzhi, Zheng, Youye, Zhang, Gangyang, and Qu, Wenjun, 2008, The first discovery of porphyry copper deposits formed during the main Indian-Tibetan collision in Gangdise, Tibet—Constraints from Re-Os ages for molybdenite from the Jiru porphyry copper deposit: Acta Geologica Sichuan, v. 28, p. 296–299. [In Chinese, with English abstract.]

Guo, Na, Chen, Jianping, Tang, Juxing, and Guo, Ke, 2010, A study of the metallogenic prognosis for the periphery of Jiama copper-polymetallic ore, Tibet, based on the RS method: Earth Science Frontiers, v. 17, p. 280–289. [In Chinese, with English abstract.]

Guo, Zhengfu, Wilson, Marjorie, and Liu, Jiaqi, 2007, Post-collisional adakites in south Tibet—Products of partial melting of subduction-modified lower crust: Lithos, v. 96, p. 205–244.

Han, Shanchu, Pan, Jiayong, Guo, Guolin, Kang, Zili, Gopng, Youxun, and Guo, Wenzheng, 2008, The study on the occurrence characteristics of ore-forming elements from the Yuejingou copper polymetallic deposit, Lasa, Tibet: Journal of East China Institute of Technology, v. 31, p. 12–19. [In Chinese, with English abstract.]

Hou, Zengqian, and Cook, Nigel J., 2009, Metallogenesis of the Tibetan collisional orogen—A review and introduction to the special issue: Ore Geology Reviews, v. 36, p. 2–24.

Hou, Zengqian, Qu Xiaoming, Wang Shuxian, Du Andao, Gao, Yongfeng, and Huang, Wei, 2004, Re-Os age for molybdenite from the Gangdese porphyry copper belt on Tibetan plateau—Implication for geodynamic setting and duration of the Cu mineralization—Science in China Series D: Earth Sciences, v. 47, no. 3, p. 221–231.

Hou, Zengqian, Yang, Zhiming, Qu, Xiaoming, Meng, Xiangjin, Li, Zhenqing, Beaudoin, G., Rui, Zongyao, Gao, Yongfeng, and Zaw, Khin, 2009, The Miocene Gangdese porphyry copper belt generated during post-collisional extension in the Tibetan Orogen: Ore Geology Reviews, v. 36, p. 25–51.

Hou, Zengqian, Zhang, Hongrui, Pan, Xiaofei, and Yang, Zhiming, 2011, Porphyry Cu (-Mo-Au) deposits related to melting of thickened mafic lower crust—Examples from the eastern Tethyan metallogenic domain: Ore Geology Reviews, v. 39, p. 21–45.

Ji, Wei Qiang, Wu, Fu Yuan, Liu, Chuan Zhou, and Chung, Sun Lin, 2009, Geochronology and petrogenesis of granitic rocks in Gangdese batholith, southern Tibet—Science in China, Series D: Earth Sciences, v. 52, p. 1240–1261.

Jiang, Huazhai, and Jiang, Shanyuan, 2006, Geological characteristics and preliminary discussion on genesis of Liebu copper deposit in Tibet: Contributions to Geology and Mineral Resources Research, v. 21(s), p. 10–14. [In Chinese, with English abstract.]

Jiang, Shenyuan, Cheng, Zikang, and Han, Fengjie, 2006, Geological characteristics and potential of Qiangdui porphyry-skarn complex copper deposit in Tibet: Contributions to Geology and Mineral Resources Research, v. 21, p. 22–26. [In Chinese, with English abstract.]

John, D.A., Ayuso, R.A., Barton, M.D., Blakeley, R.J., Bodnar, R.J., Dilles, J.H., Gray, F., Graybeal, F.T., Mars, J.C., McPhee, D.K., Seal, R.R., Taylor, R.D., and Vikre, P.G., 2010, Porphyry copper deposit model, chap. B of Mineral deposit models for resource assessment: U.S. Geological Survey Scientific Investigations Report 2010-5070-B, 169 p., accessed September 8, 2010, at http://pubs.usgs.gov/sir/2010/5070/b/.

Kamitani, M., Okumura, K., Teraoka, Y., Miyano, S., and Watanabe, Y., 2007, Mineral resources map of East Asia: Geological Survey of Japan, data sheet and explanatory notes, accessed February 8, 2010, at http://www.gsj.jp/Map/EN/docs/overseas_doc/mrm-e_asia.htm.

Kirkham, R.V., and Dunne, K.P.E., 2000, World distribution of porphyry, porphyry-associated skarn, and bulk-tonnage epithermal deposits and occurrences: Geological Survey of Canada Open File 3792a, 26 p.

Kong, Mu, Liu, Huazhong, and Yang, Shaoping, 2007, Geochemical evaluation of ore potential in the Chongjiang copper deposit and its peripheral region, Tibet: Geology and Prospecting, v. 43, p. 7–11. [In Chinese, with English abstract.]

Lang, Xinghai, Tang, Juxing, and Wang, Zizheng, 2007, Geological prospects and prospecting guide of the Zemoduola copper gold deposit in central Gandise, Tibet: Geology and Resources, v. 16, p. 29–33. [In Chinese, with English abstract.]

Leng, Chengbiao, Zhang, Xingchun, and Zho, Weide, 2010, A primary study of the geological characteristics and zircon U-Pb age of the Gangjiang porphyry copper-molybdenum deposit in Nimu, Tibet: Earth Science Frontiers, v. 17, p. 185–197. [In Chinese, with English abstract.]

Li, Guangming, Qin, Kezhang, Chen, Lei, Chen, Jinviao, Fan, Xin, and Ju, Yitai, 2011, The metallogenic model of Eocene skarn Cu-Mo-W (Au) deposits in the eastern section of Gangdese, southern Tibet, and its implication for ore—Search towards the deep subsurface: Geology and Exploration, v. 47, p. 20–30.

Li, Guangming, Qin, Kezhang, Ding, Kuishou, Li, Jinxiang, Wang, Shaohuai, Jiang, Sanyuan, Lin, Jindeng, Jiang, Huazai, Fang, Shuyan, and Zhang, Xinchun, 2006, Geology and mineral assemblage of Tertiary skarn Cu-Au±Mo deposits in the southeastern Gangdese arc—Implications for deep exploration: Acta Geologica Sinica, v. 80, p. 1407–1423. [In Chinese, with English abstract.]

Li, Guangming, Qin, Kezhang, Ding, Kuishou, and Zhang, Xingchun, 2005, Cenozoic skarn Cu-Au deposits in SE Gangdese—Features, ages, mineral assemblages, and exploration significance: Mineral Deposit Research—Meeting the Global Challenge, Proceedings of the Eighth Biennial SGA, Beijing, 2005, v. 1, p. 1239–1241.

Li, J.X., Kin, K.Z., Li, G.M., and Yang, L.K., 2007, K-Ar and 40Ar/39Ar age dating of Nimu porphyry copper orefield in Central Gangdese—Constraints on magmatic-hydrothermal evolution and metallogenic tectonic setting: Acta Petrologica Sinica, v. 23, p. 953–966. [In Chinese, with English abstract.]

Li, Shengrong, Qu, Wenjun, Yuan, Wanming, Deng, Jun, Hou, Zhengqian, and Du, Andao, 2004, Re-Os dating of the porphyry copper deposits in southern Gangdese metallogenic belt, Tibet: Himalayan Journal of Sciences, v. 2, no. 4 (special issue), p. 192–193.

Li, Yongsheng, Zhao, Caishenfg, Lü, Zhicheng, Yan, Guangsheng, and Zhen, Shimin, 2011, Characteristics of fluid inclusions in Jiama copper-polymetallic ore deposit, Tibet, and its geological significance: Journal of Jilin University (Earth Science Edition), v. 41, p. 122–136. [In Chinese, with English abstract.]

Meng, X.J., Hou, Z.Q., Gao, Y.F., Huang, W., Qu, X.M., and Qu, W.J., 2003a, Re-Os dating for molybdenite from Qulong porphyry copper deposit in Gangdese metallogenic belt, Xizang, and its metallogenic significance: Geological Review, v. 49, p. 660–666. [In Chinese, with English abstract.]

Meng, Xiangjin, Hou, Zengqian, Gao, Yongfeng, Huang, Wei, Qu, Xiaoming, and Qu, Wenjun, 2003b, Development of porphyry copper-molybdenum-lead-zinc ore-forming system in east Gangdese belt, Tibet—Evidence from Re-Os age of molybdenite in Bangpu copper polymetallic deposit: Mineral Deposits, v. 22, p. 246–252. [In Chinese, with English abstract.]

Metal Mining Agency of Japan (MMAJ), 1998, Mineral resources map of Asia: Metal Mining Agency of Japan, 1 sheet and 43 p.

Mo, Jihai, Liang, Huaying, Yu, Hengxiang, Chen, Yong, and Sun, Weidong, 2008, Zircon U-Pb age of biotite hornblende monzonitic granite for Chongmuda Cu-Au (Mo) deposit in Gangdese belt, Xizang, China, and its implications: Geochimica, v. 2008, p. 206–212. [In Chinese, with English abstract.]

Natural Resources Canada, 2010, World minerals geoscience database: accessed February 8, 2010 at http://gsc nrcan.gc.ca/wmgdb/index_e.php.

Qin, Kezhang, Li, Guangming, Zhao, Junxing, Li, Jinxiang, Xue, Guoqiang, Yan, Gang, Su, Dengkui, Xiao, Bo, Chen, Li, and Fan, Xin, 2008, Discovery of Sharang large-scale porphyry molybdenum deposit, the first single Mo deposit in Tibet and its significance: Geology in China, v. 2008, p. 1101–1112. [In Chinese, with English abstract.]

Qu, Xiaoming, Hou, Zengqian, Zaw, Khin, and Li, Youguo, 2007, Characteristics and genesis of Gangdese porphyry copper deposits in the southern Tibetan Plateau—Preliminary geochemical and geochronological results: Ore Geology Reviews, v. 31, p. 205–223.

Qu, Xiaoming, Hou, Zengqian, Zaw, Khin, Mo, Xuanxue, Xu, Wenyi, and Xin, Hongbo, 2009, A large-scale copper ore-forming event accompanying rapid uplift of the southern Tibetan plateau—Evidence from zircon SHRIMP U-Pb dating and LA ICP-MS analysis: Ore Geology Reviews, v. 36, p. 52–64.

Rebagliati, C.M., Lang, J.R., and Chisholm, I.R., 2007, Summary report on the 2006 exploration program at the Xietongmen property: accessed January 2011, at http://www.sedar.com/GetFile.do?lang=EN&docClass=24&issuerNo=00000185&fileName=/csfsprod/data83/filings/01139183/00000001/C%3A%5CSEDAR%5CFILINGS%5CKMKXietongmenTechRpt.pdf.

Rebagliati, C.M., Lang, J.R., Titley, E.D., Melis, Lawrence, Chisholm, I.R., Mosher, Greg, and Copeland, D.J., 2009, Technical report on the 2007 and 2008 exploration programs—Xietongmen property: accessed January 2011, at http://www.sedar.com/DisplayCompanyDocuments.do?lang=EN&issuerNo=00000185.

Root, D.H., Menzie, W.D., and Scott, W.A., 1992, Computer Monte Carlo simulation in quantitative resource estimation: Natural Resources Research, v. 1, no. 2, p. 125–138.

Rui, Z.Y., Hou, Z.Q., Qu, X.M., Zhang, L.S., Wang, L.S., and Liu, Y.L., 2003, Metallogenic epoch of the Gangdese porphyry copper belt and uplift of the Qinghai-Tibet plateau: Mineral Deposits, v. 22, p. 224–232. [In Chinese, with English abstract.]

Rui, Z.Y., Wang, L.S., and Zhang, L.S., 2005, Porphyry copper belts in Tibet: Mineral Deposit Research—Meeting the Global Challenge, Proceedings of the Eighth Biennial SGA, Beijing, 2005, v. 1, p. 1263–1265.

She, Hongquan, Li, Guangming, Dong, Yingjun, Pan, Guitang, Li, Jinwen, Zhang, Dequan, and Feng, Chengyou, 2009, Regional metallogenic prognosis and mineral reserves estimation for porphyry copper deposits in Gangdese polymetallic orebelt, Tibet: Mineral Deposits, v. 28, p. 803–814. [In Chinese, with English abstract.]

Singer, D.A., 2008, Mineral deposit densities for estimating mineral resources: Mathematical Geosciences, v. 40, p. 33–46.

Singer, D.A., Berger, V.I., Menzie, W.D., and Berger, B.R., 2005, Porphyry copper density: Economic Geology, v. 100, no. 3, p. 491–514.

Singer, D.A., Berger, V.I., and Moring, B.C., 2008, Porphyry copper deposits of the world: U.S. Geological Survey Open-File Report 2008–1155, 45 p., accessed August 10, 2009, at http://pubs.usgs.gov/of/2008/1155/.

Singer, D.A. and Menzie, W.D., 2005, Statistical guides to estimating the number of undiscovered mineral deposits—An example with porphyry copper deposits, *in* Cheng, Qiuming, and Bonham-Carter, Graeme, eds., Proceedings of IAMG—The annual conference of the International Association for Mathematical Geology: Toronto, Canada, Geomatics Research Laboratory, York University, p. 1028–1033.

South China Resources, 2006, Cooperative Joint Venture—Zhunuo Copper Project: unpaginated, accessed August 19, 2011, at http://www.universalcoal.com/im/press_display.php?Id=2006/27dec06.

Tafti, Reza, Mortensen, J.K., Lang, J.R., Rebagliati, Mark, and Oliver, J.L., 2009, Jurassic U-Pb and Re-Os ages for the newly discovered Xietongmen Cu-Au porphyry district, Tibet, PRC—Implications for metallogenic epochs in the southern Gangdese belt: Economic Geology, v. 104, p. 127–136.

Tang, Juxing, Wang, Denghong, Wang, Xiongwu, Zhong, Kanghui, Ying, Lijuan, Zheng, Wenbao, Li, Fengji, Guo, Na, Qin, Zhipeng, Yao, Xiaofeng, Li, Lei, Wang, You, and Tang, Xiaoqian, 2010, Geological features and metallogenic model of the Jiama copper-polymetallic deposit in Tibet: Acta Geoscientica Sinica, v. 31, p. 495–506. [In Chinese, with English abstract.]

U.S. Department of State, 2009, Small-scale digital international land boundaries (SSIB)—Lines, edition 10, and polygons, beta edition 1, *in* Boundaries and sovereignty encyclopedia (B.A.S.E.): U.S. Department of State, Office of the Geographer and Global Issues.

Wang, Gui, 2010, Study on geochemistry of fluid inclusion in Yuejingou copper polymetallic deposit: Journal of Henan Polytechnic University (Natural Science), v. 29, p. 757–765. [In Chinese, with English abstract.]

Wang, Zhihua, Wu, Xingquan, Wang, Keqiang, Yu, Wanqiang, Huang, Hui, and Ma, Dexi, 2007, Stable isotope and ore genesis of Jiagangxueshan W-Mo-Bi polymetallic deposit, Shenzha County, Tibet: Geology and Prospecting, v. 43, p. 6–10. [In Chinese, with English abstract.]

Wen, Daren, Liu, Dunyi, Chung, Sunlin, Chu, Meifei, Ji, Jianqing, Qi, Zhang, Song, Biao, Lee, Tungyi, Yeh, Mengwang, and Lo, Chinghua, 2008, Zircon SHRIMP U-Pb ages of the Gangdese Batholith and implications for Neotethyan subduction in southern Tibet: Chemical Geology, v. 252, p. 191–201.

Xia, Baoben, Xia, Bin, Wang, Baodi, Li, Jianfeng, Zhang, Xingguo, and Wang, Yingchao, 2010, Formation time of the Tangbula porphyry Mo-Cu deposit—Evidence from SHRIMP zircon U-Pb dating of Tangbula ore-bearing porphyries: Geotectonica et Metallogenia, v. 34, p. 291–297. [In Chinese, with English abstract.]

Xie, Yuling, Xu, Jiuhua, Li, Guangming, Yang, Zhiming, and Yi, Longsheng, 2007, Characteristics and evolution of ore-forming fluids of the Chongjiang copper deposit in the Gangdise porphyry copper belt, Tibet: Journal of University of Science and Technology Beijing, v. 14, p. 97–102.

Xu, Wenyi, Pan, Fengchu, Qu, Xiaoming, Hou, Zengqian, Yang, Zhusen, Chen, Weishi, Yang, Dan, and Cui, Yanhe, 2009, Xiongcun, Tibet—A telescoped system of veinlet-disseminated Cu (Au) mineralization and late vein-style Au (Ag)-polymetallic mineralization in a continental collision zone: Ore Geology Reviews, v. 36, p. 174–193.

Yan, Guangsheng, Qiu, Ruizhao, Lian, Changyun, Nokleberg, Warren J., Cao, Li, Chen Xiufa, Mao, Jingwen, Xiao, Keyan, Li, Jinyi, Xiao, Qinghui, Zhou, Su, Wang, Mingyan, Liu, Dawen, Yuan, Chunhua, Han, Jiuxi, Wang, Liangliang, Chen, Zhen, Chen, Yuming, Xie, Guiqing, and Ding, Jianhua, 2007, Quantitative assessment of the resource potential of porphyry copper systems in China: Earth Science Frontiers, v. 14, p. 27–41.

Yang, Zhiming, Hou, Zengqian, White, Noel C., Chang, Zhaoshan, Li, Zhenqing, and Song, Yucai, 2009, Geology of the post-collisional porphyry copper–molybdenum deposit at Qulong, Tibet: Ore Geology Reviews, v. 36, p. 133–159.

Yang, Zhiming, Xie, Yuling, Li, Guangming, and Xu, Jiuhua, 2006, SEM/EDS constraints on nature of ore-forming fluids in Gangdese porphyry copper belt—Case studies of Qulong and Tinggong deposits: Mineral Deposits, v. 25, p. 147–154. [In Chinese, with English abstract.]

Yang, Zhiming, Xie, Yuling, Li, Guangming, Xu, Jiuhua, and Wang, Baohua, 2005, Study of fluid inclusions from Tinggong porphyry copper deposit in Gangdese belt, Tibet: Mineral Deposits, v. 24, p. 584–594. [In Chinese, with English abstract.]

Ying, Lijuan, Wang, Denghong, Tang, Juxing, Chang, Zhesheng, Qu, Wenjun, Zheng, Wenbao, and Wang, Huan, 2010, Re-Os dating of molybdenite from the Jiama copper polymetallic deposit in Tibet and its metallogenic significance: Acta Geologica Sinica, v. 84, p. 1165–1174. [In Chinese, with English abstract.]

Zhang, Q.L., Zu, X.M., Hou, Z.Q., and Chen, W.S., 2003, Study of the fluid inclusions from Nanmu porphyry Cu-Mo deposit in Tibet: Acta Petrologica Sinica, v. 19, p. 251–259. [In Chinese, with English abstract.]

Zhang, X.G., Wang, B.D., Xia, B.B., and Qiong, Da, 2008, Discovery of the Tangbula porphyry molybdenum-copper deposit in the eastern segment of the Gangdise metallogenic belt and its significance: Geological Bulletin of China, v. 27, p. 837–843. [In Chinese, with English abstract.]

Zheng, Youye, Gao, Shunbao, Zhang, Daquan, and others, 2006, The discovery of the Zhunuo porphyry copper deposit in Tibet and its significance: Earth Science Frontiers, v. 13, p. 233–239. [In Chinese, with English abstract.]

Zheng, Youye, Duo, Ji, Cheng, Shunbo, Gao, Shunbao, and Dai, Fanghua, 2007a, Progress in porphyry copper exploration from the Gangdise belt, Tibet, China: Frontiers in Earth Science in China, v. 1, p. 226–231.

Zheng, Youye, Duo, Ji, Zhang, Gangyang, Gao, Shunbao, and Fan, Zihui, 2007b, discovery of Jiru porphyry copper deposit in Tibet and its significance: Mineral Deposits, v. 26, p. 317–321. [In Chinese, with English abstract.]

Zheng, Youye, Zhang, Gangyang, Xu, Rongke, Gao, Shunbao, Pang, Yingchun, Cao, Liang, Du, Andao and Shi, Yuruo, 2007c, Geochronologic constraints on magmatic intrusions and mineralization of the Zhunuo porphyry copper deposit in Gangdese, Tibet: Chinese Science Bulletin, v. 52, no. 22, p. 3139–3147.

Zhou, Xiong, Wen, Chunqi, Huo, Yan, Fei, Guangchun, and Wu, Pengyu, 2010, Characteristics of ore-forming fluid of Bangpu molybdenum-copper polymetallic deposit, Maizhokunggar area, Tibet, China: Geological Bulletin of China, v. 29, p. 1039–1048. [In Chinese, with English abstract.]

Zuo, Renguang, Cheng, Qiuming, and Agterberg, F. P., 2009b, Application of a hybrid method combining multilevel fuzzy comprehensive evaluation with asymmetric fuzzy relation analysis to mapping prospectivity: Ore Geology Reviews, v. 35, p. 101–108.

Zuo, Renguang, Cheng, Qiuming, Agterberg, F.P., and Xia, Qinglin, 2009a, Application of singularity mapping technique to identify local anomalies using stream sediment geochemical data, a case study from Gangdese, Tibet, western China: Journal of Geochemical Exploration, v. 101, p. 225–235.

Appendix D. Description of GIS files

An ESRI geodatabase file (TIBET_pCu.gdb) containing three feature classes and an ESRI map document (TIBET_GIS.mxd) are included with this report. These may be downloaded from the USGS website as zipped file **GIS_SIR5090F_appendix_D.zip**, which also contains the data in shapefile format.

The feature classes (and shapefiles) are as follows:

TIBET_pCu_Tracts is a vector (polygon) feature class that represents the three permissive tracts. Attributes include the tract identifiers, tract name, a brief description of the basis for tract delineation, and assessment results. Attributes are defined in the metadata that accompanies files.

TIBET _pCu_Deposits_prospects is a vector (point) feature class that represents the locations for known deposits (identified resources that have well-defined tonnage and copper grade) and prospects. The deposits and prospects are listed in tables in Appendix A, B, and C of this report. Attributes include the assigned tract, alternate site names, information on grades and tonnages, age, mineralogy, associated igneous rocks, site status, comments fields, data sources and references. Attributes are defined in the metadata that accompanies the files.

TIBET _political_boundaries is a vector (polygon) feature class that represents the political boundaries in and adjacent to the study area. The data were extracted from the country and shoreline boundaries maintained by the U.S. Department of State (2009).

The files can be viewed with an included ESRI map document (version 9.3) named **TIBET_GIS.mxd**.

Reference Cited

U.S. Department of State, 2009, Small-scale digital international land boundaries (SSIB)—Lines, edition 10, and polygons, beta edition 1, *in* Boundaries and sovereignty encyclopedia (B.A.S.E.): U.S. Department of State, Office of the Geographer and Global Issues.

Appendix E. Assessment Team

Steve Ludington is a research geologist with the USGS in Menlo Park, California. He received a B.A. in geology from Stanford University (1967) and a Ph.D. in geology from the University of Colorado (1974). He worked as an exploration geologist in Colorado, New Mexico, and Arizona before joining the USGS in 1974. His work with the USGS has included regional geologic studies, metallogenic and geochemical studies, wilderness studies, and mineral-resource assessments. He has done mineral-resource assessment work in the United States, Costa Rica, Bolivia, Mongolia, Afghanistan, and Mexico and was a coordinator for the 1998 USGS National Mineral Resource Assessment.

Jane M. Hammarstrom is a research geologist with the USGS in Reston, Virginia. She received a B.S. in geology from George Washington University in 1972 and an M.S. in geology from Virginia Polytechnic Institute and State University in 1981. She is Co-chief of the USGS Global Mineral Resource Assessment project and the task leader for the porphyry copper assessment. Jane has more than 30 years of research experience in igneous petrology, mineralogy, geochemistry, economic geology, and mineral resource assessment.

Gilpin R. Robinson, Jr. is a research geologist with the USGS in Reston, Virginia. He received a B.S. in geology from Tufts University (1973) and a Ph.D. in geology from Harvard University (1979). He is a geologist, geochemist, and mineral resources specialist working on mineral resource assessment and other projects, including geologic mapping, studies of the origin and genesis of metal and industrial mineral deposits, and geochemical modeling.

Produced in the Menlo Park Publishing Service Center, California
Manuscript approved for publication, June 27, 2012
Edited by Jane Eggleston
Layout and design by Jeanne S. DiLeo

USGS

Ludington and others—**Global Mineral Resource Assessment—Porphyry Copper Assessment of the Tibetan Plateau, China**—Scientific Investigations Report 2010-5090-F